free
to be me

stasi eldredge

free
to be *me*

becoming the young woman God created you to be

David C Cook

transforming lives together

FREE TO BE ME
Published by David C Cook
4050 Lee Vance View
Colorado Springs, CO 80918 U.S.A.

David C Cook Distribution Canada
55 Woodslee Avenue, Paris, Ontario, Canada N3L 3E5

David C Cook U.K., Kingsway Communications
Eastbourne, East Sussex BN23 6NT, England

The graphic circle C logo is a registered trademark of David C Cook.

LCCN 2014945716
ISBN 978-1-4347-0863-2
eISBN 978-1-4347-0903-5

© 2014 Stasi Eldredge
Published in association with Yates & Yates, www.yates2.com

The Team: Ingrid Beck, Karen Lee-Thorp, Amy Konyndyk, Nick Lee, Karen Athen
Cover Design: Amy Konyndyk

Printed in the United States of America
First Edition 2014

2 3 4 5 6 7 8 9 10

100614

Be who God meant you to be and you will set the world on fire.

Catherine of Siena

For girls everywhere
who will set the world ablaze in the service of Love.

contents

introduction

This book is for you if you want more.

More joy.

More freedom.

More hope.

More healing.

More life!

If you want to laugh more.

And be more kind.

Be more happy.

Be more yourself.

If you want to love more, know God more, and become more content in your own skin.

And really, who doesn't?

There is such a thing as holy dissatisfaction. It is an unsettled feeling inside that moves you not toward self-contempt but to a passionate pursuit of the God who says more is available.

I want more. I bet you do too.

Hi. I'm Stasi and, okay, yes, it's been a while since I was in middle school or high school, or even was carded while purchasing a bottle of wine as a housewarming gift. I'm in my fifties. We might as well get that out in the open right away. I'm in my fifties and I'm not your teacher, your aunt, your sister, your youth group leader, your neighbor, or your mom. And I've learned some things along the way getting to this age. I've learned from the women around me—younger and older—and some of what I've learned I want to share with you! Want to get cozy and settle in? Let me begin by sharing these ultimate words of wisdom.

It gets better.

No, really. It does. It might feel hard for a while there. Life is kind of like that, but cross my heart, I'm telling you the truth. It gets better.

You will find your way. You will grow and learn and figure it out and change in the ways you so long to. Because of Jesus. Because of Jesus, change is not only possible, it's promised.

> And we all, who with unveiled faces contemplate the Lord's glory, are being transformed into his image with ever-increasing glory, which comes from the Lord, who is the Spirit. (2 Cor. 3:18)

You are being transformed into the very image of Jesus. He who has called you is faithful, and what he has begun he will complete. You are not on your own, but you have a part to play. You must be an active participant in your own life. Jesus wants you to be free to be and offer and even enjoy who you are. Do you want this too? Then let's go forward into the book. I think it holds some beautiful treasures for you!

at a glance

I want you to read the book. I really do. Better, I'd love you to read it with a few friends and share your thoughts about it. Share your life. This isn't a book of advice; it's a book about the journey of life that you are on. Still, if you want me to give you some advice, this would be it. It would make a good poster.

Go ahead and be smart. Be strong. Be kind. Be glorious. Be courageous. Be YOU. Care for your heart. Care for your body. Allow yourself to dream. Ask questions. Break barriers. Write thank-you notes. Pursue truth. Pursue healing. Pursue Jesus.

Laugh. Explore. Pay more attention to how you feel than how you look. Tell yourself you're beautiful. Go for a walk. Daydream. Take a self-defense course. Volunteer. Be an advocate for someone in need. Find your passion. Read a book just for fun. Pray. Listen.

Find pictures in clouds. Laugh at yourself. Smile at strangers. Give large tips. Open the door for others. Say thank you when someone does it for you. Just say thank you. A lot. Respect your intuition. Practice a firm handshake. Look people in the eyes.

Ask God to reveal his love for you. Pay attention. Forgive offenses. Let people go who aren't true friends. Don't look back. Try something new. Go bowling. Go to the zoo. Fly a kite at the park. Get back on your bike. Get a bike. Pet a dog. Set a goal. Live your life. Invite someone to come along with you.

When you enjoy something, be it a fragrance, a feeling, or a view, receive it as the love note from Jesus that it is and say to him, "I love you, too."

And now, let's move away from advice giving and get into the heart of the matter. Which, by the way, is your heart.

Chapter One

the heart of the matter

*To be yourself in a world that is constantly trying to make
you something else is the greatest accomplishment.*
Ralph Waldo Emerson

*Tell me, what is it you plan to do with
your one wild and precious life?*
Mary Oliver

I am trying to get some work done, but I am dog-sitting a nine-week-old puppy. I am, shall we say, distracted. It's kind of a hassle to keep an eye on him, but he also is making me laugh harder than I have in a long time. Right now he's investigating a fake plant. His nose is buried in it, he's biting it with his sharp little puppy teeth, and every now and again he is growling at it. This puppy is 100 percent this puppy.

His name is Roper. He's a heeler and he's smart and he's learning the boundaries to live within. (No! Not there, Roper! Outside!)

He is happiness dogified. He is a joy bomb. And one of the things that makes him so absolutely marvelous is that he is not trying to be anything other than what he is. He is a puppy. He's not a kitten. He's not a gerbil. He's not an older dog. He is Roper. The nine-week-old version. And that is a very good thing. Because that is exactly who he's supposed to be.

He is supposed to be himself. I am supposed to be me.

You're supposed to be you.

Self-assured is not how anyone would have described me in high school. Confident. Self-possessed. Fearless. I may have looked that way. I sure tried hard to appear that way. I was nice. But if there had been a sign hanging over my heart, it would have read, "Just tell me who I'm supposed to be and I'll be that." My parents had an idea of who I was supposed to be. (Smarter! Thinner! More popular!) My friends were quite willing to tell me, without even speaking, who I was supposed to be. (Funnier! Prettier!) I let my sisters tell me who I was supposed to be. I sure let boys tell me.

I let other people tell me who I was and who I was not before I even had a clue as to whether or not they were right.

We don't come into this world with a grand sense of self. Or maybe we do. Maybe we are assured as a newborn and then life chips away at our innate sense of unique well-being. Life happens, things happen, words are spoken, and it isn't very long before we figure out that in order to survive, there is a person we need to be, and she isn't us. Not truly. Not fully. Not freely.

Just tell me who I am supposed to be and I'll be that.

Big sigh.

(Roper has now collapsed at my feet and is sleeping. He just let out a big puppy dream sigh. We are sighing together.)

Life can be really lonely.

So I bet you can guess what I'm going to say next, right? I'm going to tell you that in order to have a life worth living, you need to be you! You're correct.

In order to have a life worth living, you need to be you. Not the parental- or friend- or boy-dictated version. Not the Internet-updated version. But the true version.

You are you. You actually can't be anyone else. God made you you on purpose. You are the only one alive who ever was or ever will be you. "Today you are you! That is truer than true! There is no one alive who is you-er than you!" said the brilliant Dr. Seuss.[1] You is not only who you get to be; it's who you are supposed to be.

Problems come when we would rather be someone else. Anyone else. Sometimes others don't like us. Sometimes we don't like ourselves. We know where we are struggling or failing or hurting or simply wanting out. We know we are not all that we are meant to be.

So here's the good news. You are meant to be you, but you are meant to become a better you. You are meant to change and grow in the ways you long to. That is, in fact, why you long to.

The very fact that we long for the change we do is a sign that we are meant to have it. Our very dissatisfaction with our weaknesses and struggles points to the reality that continuing to live in them is not our destiny. Read those two sentences again.

See, that's what life is all about. Moving forward and upward and becoming the next higher version of yourself, always. But not merely by your own efforts. Not by a strength of will or a bitter form of self-discipline or a rigorous regime of self-loathing. But through the love of God.

I want to grow. I want to change. I want to become more true, more loving, more authentic, more me. Jesus wants that too. He wants you to become more you, too! Jesus loves who you are. He sees you and knows you and thinks you're amazing. He also knows who you are meant to be, and by his love and grace he wants to partner with you on your journey.

from the heart

Life is a journey of becoming the true you. Which means, it is a journey of the heart.

We have to begin with the heart because that is where all the true action is. Your heart is central. It's been battered, and there will be times when it will be battered again. It can cause you great pain and can get you into even greater trouble. You'll be tempted to lock it away, put it on a shelf, numb it, or maybe even kill it. Certainly, there will be times when you lose it. But the thing is, you can't truly live without your heart. And you are meant to live.

Your heart is, in fact, the most important thing about you. Your heart is also the most important thing to God.

Surprise! Actually, that's really good news. Jesus came for your heart. To ransom, rescue, and restore the true you. He hasn't been moving heaven and earth through all eternity so that you would behave yourself. Fit into the crowd. Mind your manners. No. He wants to woo and win your heart for himself so that you will love him with it and live your life from it.

That's crazy good news.

I thought the journey of my life was about getting my act together, blowing it less frequently, and being a good girl. Serving people. Obeying. Following the rules. I thought that's what mattered most to God. Boy, was I wrong.

> Above all else, guard your heart, for everything you
> do flows from it. (Prov. 4:23)

Above all else, we are told, guard your heart. And guard not like a watchdog, fearfully keeping it in line, but guard as in tend, protect, and nurture. Most of us don't do that. Most of us watch over the number on the scale more closely than we do our hearts. And that is not a wise thing to do because a life without heart is not worth living, and your life matters. Your heart matters.

Above all else, watch over your heart. Seriously? Why? Because as my husband wrote in *Waking the Dead*:

> God knows that our heart is core to who we are. It is
> the source of all creativity, courage, and conviction. It is
> the fountainhead of our faith, our hope, and of course,
> our love. This "wellspring of life" within us is the very
> essence of our existence, the center of our being. Your
> heart is the most important thing about you. You can't
> become who you are meant to be without it.[2]

Remember in Genesis, God said, "'Let us make mankind in our image.' … In the image of God he created them; male and female he created them" (Gen. 1:26–27). You are made in the image of the Trinity! Have you ever wondered, "Where is that image?"

You are made in the image of God in your whole being, but primarily in your heart! You have been created female by God's design. It's his intention that you carry his image to the world as a woman in your feminine heart. Your feminine heart has been created with the greatest of all possible dignities—as a reflection of God's own heart. You are feminine to the very core of your being.

And that is what Jesus has come to restore.

So, when I speak about the heart, I am not speaking about your feelings, your emotions. You do feel deeply with the heart, but you think deeply there as well. When I speak of the heart, I am talking about the place where Christ dwells in you, by faith. The center of you. The core place inside where you are your most true self.

Okay, okay. You may be thinking, *Stasi is nuts.* You may have been taught that the heart is deceitfully wicked. That's from Jeremiah 17:9: "The heart is deceitful above all things, and desperately sick; who can understand it?" (ESV). Yes, the heart is wicked before salvation. But when a person believes in her heart that Jesus is the Son of God come to save her, and she surrenders herself to God, giving him his rightful place in her heart, she gets a new one! "I will give you a new heart and put a new spirit in you; I will remove from you your heart of stone and give you a heart of flesh" (Ezek. 36:26).

See, God knows where the problems lie, and he has come to deal with them. He knows we need his help to live well and to love well. He knows our fallen hearts are deceitfully wicked, and he made arrangements for them to not stay that way.

Therefore, if anyone is in Christ, the new creation
has come: The old has gone, the new is here! (2 Cor.
5:17)

When you become a Christian, you get a new heart.

As believers with new hearts, we still struggle with sin. Yes. We
are called to crucify our flesh every day. But we are not called to
crucify our heart. We are called to guard it.

So to begin:

Your heart matters most to God.
Your heart needs protecting.
You need to be nice to it.

We can be so mean to ourselves, can't we? We say things to ourselves that we would never say to another human being. We can be
harsh. (We see our flaws clearly, but it's much more difficult to see
our goodness, right?) Here's the thing: You need to be kind to yourself so that you will be kind to others. Because the way you treat your
heart is the way you will treat everyone else's. That's how it works.

I recently had the honor and the sorrow (yes, at the same time)
of being at the memorial service for my friend's twenty-four-year-
old son.

The service was holy. And I do mean *h.o.l.y.* Grieving his passing.
Celebrating his life. Thanking God for the truth that there is a day
coming when all will be restored. No more good-byes. Ever.

At his service, nothing was shared about how he did or did not
pick up his room. If he made his bed. Put his clothes away. Nothing

about how old he was when he got his driver's license. Not a word about his grades, his roles, or his titles.

Tons were shared about how people felt in his presence. There were lots of stories about his sense of humor. Words flowed about how he *loved* people, how he lived passionately from his heart and the joy he brought by being and offering his unique, quirky, imperfect, wonderful, on-the-road self.

It was his heart that mattered. And it's yours that matters.

So how are you doing today? How's your heart? How are you treating your heart? Are you being kind? Encouraging? Loving? To yourself? Jesus wants you to be. We are commanded to love our neighbors *as ourselves.* The thing is, we will. We will love others as we love ourselves. So if we are harsh to ourselves, we will be harsh to others whether we want to be or not. It will leak out.

Jesus loves you. He thinks you're worth protecting, pursuing, guarding, investing in, and giving his life for. He wants you to love you too, even while being keenly aware of areas in your life that you want to change.

> *Take a moment now and thank God for your life. Ask for his help to love yourself.*

becoming

My friend Julie was being faithful to her new fitness regime. She went for her prescribed run even though it was raining. She felt like she was slogging along yet one more time when another runner passed her, leaping like a gazelle. *Maybe fitness is only for the fit,* she thought. *God,* she cried out, *change is so hard!* She heard his reply deep in her heart. *What if change is actually just me unveiling who you really are?*

Wait—what?

I thought we basically got rid of ourselves, one way or another, and Jesus sort of took over and lived our life for us. Didn't John the Baptist say, "He must become greater; I must become less" (John 3:30)?

This is the paradox of our change. On the one hand, it involves surrendering ourselves to God, giving everything over to him— including all our efforts to change and all our resignation that we'll never change. As C. S. Lewis said, "Until you have given up your self to Him you will not have a real self."[3]

And yet God does not then toss us aside. He restores us—the real us. As he heals our inner life, he calls us to rise to the occasion of our lives. Once we surrender ourselves, he gives us back our true selves. In fact, the most important journey any person will take is the journey into becoming herself through the love of God. It is a journey of the heart that will require courage, faith, and above all a willingness to grow and to let go. The journey is one of increased self-awareness coupled with a surrender of self.

It is a beautiful paradox that the more God's we become, the more ourselves we become—the self he had in mind when he thought of you before the creation of the world. She's in there, girls; she might be badly bruised and covered with all sorts of muck, but she's in there. And Jesus comes to call her out. The path is a dance between choosing and yielding, desiring and relinquishing, trying and giving up.

We discover as we grow that there are tools that are not helping us along our way, but that are hurting us.

shame and discipline won't cut it

First, shame is not an agent of change.

Like a shot of caffeine in the morning, self-loathing may propel us onto the road of change, but we will find that hatred of self only leads us onto a never-ending roundabout. Like being terrified by a number on the scale in the morning and vowing never to overeat again, a shot of shame may get us through to lunch but never through to our freedom. Self-hatred, shame, and fear—though rampant in so many of our hidden worlds—are simply never going to be capable of creating or sustaining the growth we long for. Yet most of us try to use shame as our inner motivator. I know I have.

> *Have you ever used shame to motivate yourself? Are you still using it? If so, what does that voice of shame tell you? What is it trying to motivate you to do? (By shame, I am referring to an inner dialogue in which you berate yourself for not being or doing what you consider to be the right thing.)*

Shame does not lead us to God. It actually drives us further away from his kind, merciful, and good heart. Shame is not a sign of repentance, nor will it usher in the growth we long for. We do become even more ourselves as we repent of areas in our lives that have nothing to do with faith or love, but God does not live in a perpetual state of disappointment over who we are. Berating ourselves for our flaws and our weakness only serves to undermine our strength to become.

Repenting from our sin is essential. Beating ourselves up for sinning is no longer an option.

Second, self-discipline isn't going to cut it either.

Discipline, particularly spiritual discipline, is a holy and good thing, one that increases over a lifetime of practice. But when we lean on it alone to bring about the change we long for, we find that the fruit is not a grace-filled young woman. We get angry; we get discouraged. If we do make it through a few battles, we can easily become the kind of girl who pressures others to do the same, a hard and get-your-act-together kind of young woman.

With self-discipline, the focus remains "self," so we are already off to a bad start. Trying, striving, working harder may get us through the week, but it won't take us through the decades. Yet most Christians believe that this is the way to handle our external world.

Have you created lists for yourself about the ways you want to be living? Are you able to follow through with those lists?

True transformation cannot be forced from the outside. It's an inside-out process. Have you ever made a list of ways to live, eat, exercise, study, seek God, grow, and change? How long did it last? Those lists don't work very long for anyone, and so we fall back into self-contempt. The problem does not lie with our lack of discipline. The problem is in the approach. The problem lies with the lists.

By the way, we humans are great ones for making lists. Codes of behavior. Rules of etiquette. Cover your mouth when you yawn. Keep your napkin on your lap. Don't talk while you are eating. Chew with your mouth closed. Don't interrupt. Raise your hand. Wait your turn. Stand up straight.

Aren't you tired just reading this?

What else is on your list of how to behave?

God gave Israel a fabulous list. Do not lie. Do not steal. Do not covet your neighbor's wife, servant, ox, donkey, or new boots. Was it really too much to ask? Noble as the list was, the people found they couldn't keep it for a day.

Enter Jesus. In his famous Sermon on the Mount, Jesus taught that it is the life of the heart that matters. He taught that hating a person in your heart was the same as murdering that person. Ummmm, we are all in trouble here.

A list of laws, rules, tips, techniques, and strategies does not a transformed heart make. Yes, we all have areas in our lives we want and need to change, but the only way that is going to happen is when we have a change of heart.

Scrooge had a change of heart, so he gave Bob Cratchit a raise. Cinderella had a change of heart, so she went to the ball. Raging Saul the Pharisee had a change of heart, so he became missionary number one for Jesus. I had a change of heart when I surrendered my life and

gave it over to Jesus. When my heart came home to its true Home, a
lot of change instantly happened.

When we have a change of heart on the inside, it manifests itself
on the outside. But you and I both know by now that most of our
healing and changing doesn't happen at the moment of our conver-
sion. We walk it out. God invites us into a process. Our journey to get
there takes place in the day in and day out of the dusty and gritty here
and now. And it is to the dusty, gritty here and now that Jesus comes.

So shame isn't gonna do it, and discipline isn't gonna do it. God
invites us to join him in the process whereby he heals our inner world
so he can transform our outer world. The process of deep, from-the-
heart healing, growth, transformation, and freedom begins when *we
believe we are loved.*

Like you, I have areas in my life that I want and need to change.
But I've learned the freeing truth that God is not going to love me
any more or any differently when I do. Not when I finally lose the
extra weight I need to and keep it off, not when I exercise regularly,
not even when I am kinder, nicer, and more organized. Jesus's love
for me, my Father's love for me, never changes. Yeah, okay, fellowship may be strained at times, but his heart toward me does not
change. He is passionately in love with me. Even better, I think he
likes me. And by the way, he's got a pretty huge thing for you, too.
Yes, you. Right now.

The voice of shame says, *I basically hate me; I need to get rid of me.*
The voice of discipline says, *I've got to fix me because me is not good.*
God says, *I love you; let me restore you.* I like that one best.

God is *unveiling* who we truly are. Unveiled faces, as Paul put it.
All those veils of shame and sin and the false self, all those veils others

have put upon us, thinking they know who we ought to be—God takes them all away so that with unveiled faces we might reflect his glory.

> And we all, who with unveiled faces contemplate the Lord's glory, are being transformed into his image with ever-increasing glory, which comes from the Lord, who is the Spirit. (2 Cor. 3:18)

Who do you want to become? What do you want to be like? Ask God to begin to breathe hope into your heart that you can actually become her.

together

Does anybody ever really change? From the heart? I believe they do. I've seen it happen; the Scriptures promise it can happen; it's happening in me.

I am growing in believing that I am completely loved in this moment and that God isn't waiting for me to get my act together in order to become worthy of his affection. I have only and ever been lovely to God, and so have you. In the steady face of his love, I am changing.

I know you have hoped for change in the past. Today, God is inviting you to hope again. By *faith*. We cannot heal ourselves or free ourselves or save ourselves. We cannot become ourselves all by ourselves. But we are not by ourselves. We are seen and known and strengthened and urged on to the life we were created for by the King of Love. He wants to help us change and grow. We can't do it, but *he can*. He's very, very good at it. It is, in fact, what he has promised to do.

> For God knew his people in advance, and he chose them to become like his Son, so that his Son would be the firstborn among many brothers and sisters. (Rom. 8:29 NLT)

Here is what I've learned:

> Puppies are adorable and have very sharp teeth.
> We are loved beyond telling.
> There are *reasons* why we struggle with the things we do.
> God made you *you* on purpose.

Chapter Two

what's your story?

If you've heard this story before, don't stop me,
because I'd like to hear it again.

Groucho Marx

Once upon a time, there was a young maiden who lived in the center of the woods. What she was doing there, she did not know, for you see, of all the lovely things that filled her cottage, her memory was not among them.

Don't you like a good story? Stories are the language of the heart. That's why Jesus told so many stories. He is not only the bravest person you will ever meet; he is also the most brilliant. He uses stories.

The Bible doesn't read like a phone book.

You were born into a story. Your life is a story! It's the story of how your heart has been handled and what you have come to believe about yourself as a result. Do you know? You need to. You need to remember. So do I.

Forgetting my life—my mistakes, my victories, my challenges, my sorrows, my *story*—prevents me from moving forward and growing into the woman I am supposed to be. I must remember. I invite you to join me in remembering. It may seem strange that at certain points on our journey we need to look back in order to move forward, but it's true.

The temptation is to look back with regret rather than with mercy. But God's eyes see clearly, and they are filled with mercy. We can be merciful too.

It's not that I remember everything clearly. It comes to me unbidden, my history, in a fragrance I catch on the breeze, in the sound of the birds happily going about their joyous business of finding things to eat. It is a hint of eternity on the wind, a connection to seasons past, the memory of wonder, of longing, of knowing. I am still three and seven and sixteen.

crickets

The soundtrack for the first ten years of my life is crickets and thunderstorms and the sound of autumn leaves crunching beneath my feet and releasing their earthy fragrance. I grew up in a neighborhood without fences and filled with children. We explored "the ditch." We caught fireflies and put them in a mason jar. Really. We did this. It isn't just in the movies. We played Red Rover, Red Rover and Starlight, Star Bright and put on musicals for our parents.

There were four seasons, with ice skating on a real frozen lake in the winter and swimming in the public pool all summer long.

We carved pumpkins at Halloween and went trick-or-treating unescorted, safe to go into a stranger's home to get our picture taken. There were lemonade stands and sledding, tornado drills and bike riding, Sunday Mass and come-home snacks.

At six years old, while I was sick in bed with the chickenpox, I got the news I had won a newspaper coloring contest. What joy! I still have the photo my mother took when she told me of my victory. I'm smiling, sitting up next to my Pebbles doll, missing teeth on prominent display. My prize was a gift certificate to a candy store and the thrill of being chosen. Oh yes. I remember.

My mother made dinner for us every night. Every single night. Dinners out as a family were a rare extravagance reserved for New Year's Eve and the occasional road trip. "How much money can we spend?" we asked as we poured over the mystery of the menu. My mother didn't wear pearls, but she did wear an apron. And if she wasn't playing bridge, volunteering at the church, or cleaning the house, she could be found in our kitchen.

Most days, after coming home from school, I parked myself in front of the television. I can still sing jingles from commercials that are forty years old. I don't remember having a lick of homework.

My, have things changed. I'll bet that when you were ten, your mother didn't wear an apron. (What did she wear?) Maybe you had homework in fourth grade, and soccer or dance lessons. (What did you do after school?) When you were eight, did you eat at a dinner table with your family, or in the car, or in front of a television or computer? Do you remember any shows? Commercials? Favorite games?

When I was sixteen, I thought my childhood was awesome. The first time I considered the possibility that my family wasn't perfect, I felt the earth shift beneath my feet.

It's important to remember. But it's also very important to remember *honestly*. (At least when we are ready and equipped by God to do so.)

When I am honest, the soundtrack of my childhood is also the clink of ice cubes and the smell of scotch. It is the sound of barbed words flung between my parents with deadly accuracy and belts being snapped in preparation for a spanking. It is the numbing dullness wafting from the television and the sound of beer cans being opened. It is the feeling of an anxious stomach, a lonely heart, and the unfulfilled desire to be played with. It is the tangible ache of wanting to be accepted, approved of, and enjoyed. It is the sense of failing miserably.

In the ongoing remembering of my own story, God is revealing reality. It's been a journey into loss and sorrow and intense pain. It has included becoming very angry. And slowly, ever so slowly, but ever so surely, it has involved mercy, forgiveness, healing, and love.

My childhood was not idyllic. Since no one's was, I'm guessing it's a pretty safe bet your life hasn't been perfect either. But a deeper understanding of our stories leads to a deeper understanding of ourselves—who we are and who God has made us to be. Yes, there is sorrow there, but there is glory, too.

How would you describe the soundtrack of your childhood up to age ten? What are the sounds you like to remember? What are the ones you don't like to remember?

shaped by childhood

The first ten years of a person's life pass all too quickly, but the effect of them colors the rest of her life. Whether mostly good or mostly awful, most childhoods are a mixture of both. They are meant to be years free and unencumbered by weighty adult issues. These are the wonder years, the years of blowing bubbles, drawing on the sidewalk with chalk, and finding whales in the clouds. Marked by exploration, the sound of swing sets, and the smell of dandelions, these formative years are the foundation for the rest of our lives.

What were your first ten years like? What did you like? What games did you enjoy? Were *you* enjoyed? Do you feel enjoyed today?

What were you like as a little girl? Take a few moments and remember. Describe yourself as a little girl. (Pretty, lively, lonely, scared ...)

Spend a few moments in silence before God. Ask him how he would describe you as a little girl. What do you sense he is saying?

What is one of your favorite childhood memories?

The youngest of five daughters, Annie grew up in rural Minnesota, surrounded by open space and extended family. Her blonde hair and blue eyes fit right in with her Dutch sisters, but her weak and ill little body did not. Annie had severe asthma that prevented her from participating in sports or neighborhood pickup games of soccer. Gripped by unrelenting fear at bedtime, she spent most nights on her parents' bedroom floor. The allergies that plagued her kept her from gaining weight and breathing deeply and living with abandon. Annie describes her little-girl self as sickly, skinny, and lonely.

How do athletic parents devoted to their active children convey love and approval to an unathletic, sickly, uninvolved child? Annie did not grow up feeling enjoyed. She did not fit into her family. Annie felt that her parents didn't know what to do with her, so they didn't do anything.

Left to herself more often than not, one of the defining wounds of her life came from the hands of a cousin. Left unattended and unprotected for hours upon hours, Annie was sexually abused. As is the story with too many girls (and guys), the effect of being violated was that Annie believed she was not worth protecting, not worth attending to, not really worth anything at all. *There is something wrong with me*, she believed.

What was your childhood like? What did you love, dream of, play, feel, believe? Invite Jesus into your memory and into your perception of it.

Dear one, if you are being abused in any way, sexually or otherwise, please know first that it's not your fault. You aren't the cause for another person's sin. And second, please tell a safe adult. You may feel as if there are no adults you can trust, but please trust someone. Someone outside of your situation. This is not how you are supposed to be treated and it needs to stop. You are worth fighting for and protecting.

be more, be less

My siblings and I used to torture each other in tickle fights. Not play—torture.

I have two sisters and one brother, and I am the youngest, so both my experience and my memory of my childhood vary vastly from theirs. We get together these days and share stories that we remember very differently. I was ten years old when my father stopped drinking; my brother was fourteen, my sisters sixteen and seventeen. A few years later my father was diagnosed with bipolar disorder and began to take the medicine that stabilized his emotions. But by that time, my sisters had left home and my brother had left in every other way he could. So as I said, their experience of childhood and the teen years varies much from my own.

But I do know that in the tickle fights, whoever was pinned to the ground would be tickled until they couldn't breathe, usually with a damp sponge gagging their mouth. Or perhaps a dirty sock.

Why do we do these things?

We had a family song. If we got together this afternoon, my siblings and I could sing it to you in perfect harmony: "It Was Only an Old Beer Bottle." Now what does that tell you about our family? I will tell you that whoever opened my father's beer can was rewarded with the first sip. At three years old I vied for the privilege. I still like the taste of it.

> *It was only an old beer bottle,*
> *A-floating on the foam.*
> *It was only an old beer bottle,*

A million miles from home.
And in it was a message
With these words written on:
Whoever finds this bottle
Will find the beer all gone. (Beeeeer allllll gooooone.)

So we were a singing family. Sort of. And though I am confident
of my siblings' love for me, while we were growing up we weren't
exactly allies. We weren't enemies either. Our alliances shifted.

Still, though we lived together and felt the same unspoken threat
of impending disaster, we were alone. Alone in the way we coped
with the mess of our parents' marriage and the message we were each
given: *you are a profound disappointment in who you are.* You need to,
why can't you—the list is endless. Weigh less. Be more tan. Be more
athletic. Be more involved. Be popular. Play sports. Play golf. Play
the piano. Be more. Be less. Be *different*.

diets

The first diet my mother put me on was when I was in the fourth
grade. I was eight years old and a wee bit chubby. School lunches
consisted of celery sticks and Buddig lunch meat. Oh, for those
lucky ones who got the little bags of potato chips or—bliss—a
Hostess something in their lunches!

I lost the seven pounds I needed to lose with much praise and
applause, and there you have it. Studies show that if you put a
person on a low-calorie-diet regime, they will lose a few pounds,
yes. But their bodies will acclimate to the regime, and they will

struggle to varying degrees with keeping their weight in a normal range from then on. Diet to lose weight, and you get hooked.

My father's work was in the fashion industry. Uh-oh. His wife's and his children's appearance was paramount. My mother had a fabulous figure. She never believed it, was constantly on one diet or another, and tried to "help" us too. Intent on my being thin, my parents sent me to a dietician when I was in the tenth grade. I had to keep a log of what I ate, learn about nutrition, and weigh in every week. I was fifteen years old. I was five feet, seven inches tall. I weighed 140 pounds.

I look at pictures of me growing up, bracing myself to see the fat, homely girl I was, and there looking back at me is a pretty, unsure-of-herself, but totally normal-weighing little girl. What was the deal? By some grace of God I didn't become anorexic or bulimic, but I did seek comfort in food. Though for many years, only a little. The secret extra four cookies, from the freezer so Mom wouldn't notice.

My mother wanted me to be more than she thought I was, more than she thought she was. Who we both were, clearly, was not enough. And too much.

Mom, looking at my hair askance: "Jenny wears her hair so stylishly, you don't even notice that she's overweight." Wallis Simpson's mantra, "A woman can never be too rich or too thin," was gospel. At least the thin part. The less you weigh, the more value you have.

As I sought solace for my heart in promiscuity my last two years of high school, my weight began to rise. Fifteen pounds in high school might as well have been fifty. So I had my two years of being truly overweight. Miserable.

When I went off to college, I discovered the power of amphetamines and in two months lost more weight than I needed to lose. But I still saw myself as the "fat girl." Unwanted. Unattractive. Ready to tip the scale into rejection at any moment. I felt I was a disappointment to my parents, never able to attain an unspoken but deeply felt level of acceptance. My siblings and I never felt we measured up.

And God was there.

God was there

My family moved from Kansas to California when I was ten years old, and thirty years later I had the opportunity to go back. As I drove slowly to the old neighborhood, I asked God to show me that he had been there for me. Pulling up in front of my well-remembered, well-loved childhood home, he answered. There, standing guard on the front porch, was a large statue of a lion. The Lion of Judah whispered to my heart that he had been standing guard the entire time. I parked the car and walked up the street to my elementary school. It was there that a few teachers had singled me out for their attention and nourished my famished heart.

"I know you were here, God. But can you show me?" The school had become a church. I was able to walk in and down the hall to my last classroom. I peeked in the windows, and there on the board, written as big as life, were the words, "God loves you."

Oh yeah, he was there.

He was there for Annie too. When she was thirty years old, God invited Annie to remember. And remember she did. She remembered her sorrow, her loneliness, her pain. And then she remembered something else. As a little girl, Annie loved the springtime. When winter would finally release its grip on her world, Annie would put on her boots and head out to the swamp near her home. It wasn't full of quicksand, but it was filled with mud. At the first sign of spring it was filled with something else as well. Buttercups. Pale yellow, tender, intricate, tiny proclaimers of beauty, buttercups would cover the swamp in wonder. A simple flower, buttercups bestow their loveliness only to muddy swamps. Buttercups do not grow in fields of fertilized grasslands. They do not display their presence on country hillsides. They only flourish in mud.

Annie's childhood was muddy. And honestly, she is one of the most beautiful women I have ever been privileged to know. Beauty for ashes. Praise for despair. The phoenix rises, and Annie has risen too with a faith that is precious and contagious and lovely beyond words. She is Jesus's very own Buttercup. Yes, God was there. He is still there.

Annie's childhood was muddy, and so was mine. There were times when yours was too. And God was there for you, too. Calling. Providing. Shielding. Aching. Loving. Why did he allow certain things to happen? I don't know. We won't know until we get to ask him face-to-face. But we do know that he is good and he is for us.

Paul wrote, "And we know that in all things God works for the good of those who love him, who have been called according to his purpose" (Rom. 8:28). One day we will understand completely. For this moment, though, we are being invited to see with his eyes of mercy.

Ask Jesus about your first ten years. Ask him to reveal to you places in your past where he was loving you, protecting you, and wooing you to himself. "Were you there, God? Where? How?"

what are we doing with it?

Every human being has some vital place in her life where she is not living in the victory she longs for, and it colors how she views herself. Every person's personal struggle rooted in her past, be it a deep-rooted self-hatred or a pressing need to control her world, makes her desperate for God. We all have something that brings us to our knees. It isn't something we would ever choose for ourselves or wish on anyone else, but we all have an area—or ten—in our lives that drives us to need God. We can't free ourselves. We are weak, aware that something inside is broken and starving. It is a wonderful grace when we finally give up and fall down before the One who is strong.

And, my friend, it is not a bad thing that you desperately need Jesus. For some reason, we feel embarrassed by our desperation. We see desperation as a sign that something is terribly wrong with us. Oh no. We were created to desperately need Jesus. We have always needed him, and we always will. I do not believe God causes the pain in our lives, but I do know that he uses it to drive us to him. The desperation is a good thing. As George MacDonald wrote,

> How many helps Thou giv'st to those would learn!
> To some sore pain, to others a sinking heart;

To some a weariness worse than any smart;
To some a haunting, fearing, blind concern …
To some a hunger that will not depart.[1]

In what areas are you desperate for God? What are the areas that you are struggling in and would love to change? When did they begin? Ask Jesus to reveal them to you and to give you his power and strength to free and heal you.

I am a hungry woman. I am hungry for love, for acceptance, for belonging, for meaning. I am desperate for God. I am aware of the aching abyss inside me of which many have written.

Oswald Chambers wrote, "There is only One being who can satisfy the last aching abyss of the human heart, and that is the Lord Jesus Christ."[2] I know that now. But I certainly didn't know it as a little girl hungry for approval and love. I didn't wake every morning and skip around the house knowing that Jesus is the One who will satisfy the starving places in my heart. I have grown into knowing it. I continue to grow into knowing it.

I wasn't even aware of how hungry I was when as a newlywed I first began to give my heart away to the drive-through. I didn't know I was making a deal with bondage. Food would satisfy my hunger, my loneliness, my ache for a while. But only for a little while. And then I would need another fix. I would get another fix, and then I got into a fix that I have spent the better part of thirty years trying to get out of.

The messages I received growing up, and particularly my mother's fixation on my weight, set me up for the struggle. The way had been paved for food to hold a power in my life it was never meant to. Obsession with the number on the scale and the size of the clothes turned over the measurement of my value as a woman to my weight and appearance.

My bondage to bingeing has shaped my life as profoundly as any other thing or person. What I came to believe about myself through my helpless state (failure) and how I chose to fight through my shame and still show up and offer what I could to others—those things shaped my soul. Witnessing the way my husband's heart was broken and transformed through *my* losing battle with food is a massively defining part of my story. A large portion of it. An extra-large portion of it. (Yes, I get the pun.)

toward healing

In my anguish and despair, I hit my knees and turn my face to Jesus again and again and again. My cries for help have been agonizing groans laden with self-loathing, accusation, and desperation. And God has met me. In the midst of overwhelming shame not merely over my body but my self, God has drawn me to his heart and spoken to me Truth. He speaks Love and Truth, right in the middle of my pain and the familiar voices screaming my failure.

Part of our healing comes with forgiveness (of ourselves and others), and part of it comes with repentance. But first, we have to begin with how God sees us. How he sees you. Do you know?

You are deeply and completely loved (Rom. 8:38–39).

You are totally and completely forgiven (1 John 2:12).

When God sees you, he sees the righteousness of Jesus (2 Cor. 5:21).

You mean the whole world to him (John 3:16).

He thinks you are beautiful. Right now (Song of Sol. 4:1).

He is committed to your restoration (Rom. 8:29).

You are not now, nor have you ever been, alone (Heb. 13:5).

Choose one of the above statements. Do you believe it? Really? Deep down? What helps you believe it? What gets in the way?

forgiveness

Let me say a word or two about forgiveness. Forgiveness is crucial if we are to look at our stories in mercy. Forgiveness, like repentance, is essential and an act of our will. It is also a commandment from our God. When we forgive others, we are not saying that what they did was all right. No. We are saying that we will not hold on to our pain, our rage, or our sense of injustice any longer. We release them to God to deal with, and we refuse to let them hurt us any longer.

Are there people you need to forgive? Ask God for his help to forgive them.

My struggle with my weight is only a part of my story. Yes, it is a large part and frames more than two decades of my life, but God has used it to draw my heart to him. I don't believe he has caused it. But I know that he has used it. And I choose to forgive my mother. I forgive my father. I even forgive myself. Again.

Though our past has shaped us, we are not our past. Though our failures and sin have had an effect on who we are, we are not defined by our failures or our sin. Though thought patterns and addictions may have overwhelmed us, we are not overcome by them, and we will never be overcome by them. Jesus has won our victory. Jesus is our victory.

The stories from our past that shaped us and the words that were spoken over our lives that have crippled us do not stand a chance in the light of the powerful grace and mercy that come to us now in the person of Jesus. Yes, God uses our stories to shape us. He works all things for the good of those who love him, even the horrible things. The holy work of God deep in our hearts as we have suffered and struggled and wept and longed to overcome is stunning beyond measure. You may not see the goodness yet, but you will. You will. It comes when we see our lives through God's eyes.

Jesus is inviting us to recover those parts of ourselves that we have tried to hide or lop off in hopes of being more acceptable. God wants us to love him with all of our hearts, including the portions of our personalities we would like to change, the dreams long buried, and the wounds we have ignored.

God is coming. He has not abandoned us, and he never will. Yes, the pain of life is sometimes too intense to be borne. But when from that place we cry out to Jesus to save us, the heavens rejoice, the demons tremble in defeat, and the Holy Spirit, who is closer than our skin, transforms us.

Chapter Three

the landscape of your life

What lies behind us and what lies before us are tiny
matters compared to what lies within us.

Ralph Waldo Emerson

Yesterday morning I wanted to buy a puppy; this afternoon I wondered how many years I would get for homicide.

Am I simply nuts? Is this just the sin nature the Bible talks about, and I'm stuck with repenting of it again and again? No, my dear. There is an internal reality playing havoc with my world, but it is neither woundedness, nor sin, nor immaturity; not even a touch of insanity. There are powerful feminine tides washing to and fro inside each of us, and they are having an enormous influence on our lives—and on the way we perceive our lives.

Too many girls and women are unaware of how their hormones are affecting their lives—emotionally, physically, and spiritually. But we don't need to remain uninformed any longer or wonder if at certain times in our lives (or month) we are simply going crazy.

The bodies we live in and the amazing hormones that shift and flow through them help set the stage of the experience of our lives. Let's take a look at what's going on.

four seasons

The bodies of women mirror nature. Every year we have spring, summer, autumn, and winter—four beautiful seasons that will continue until the end of our time. In the same way, there are four seasons (menstrually speaking) to a woman's life and four weeks to her cycle, but they are not always neatly separate. Some women's cycles are as irregular as an unscrupulous politician's voting record, and some women's cycles function like a Swiss clock. Either way, we need to understand and honor what is going on with our bodies.

Let's start with the four seasons.[1] First we have preadolescence when our body develops at a rapid and sometimes awkward rate. These years set the foundation of our self-perception. Our heart's deepest questions are being answered. *Am I loved? Am I worth loving? Am I captivating?* From infants to toddlers to little girls, we are becoming ourselves, developing into womanhood. In this season, we are fully feminine and are not yet encumbered (or blessed) by our period.

The next season of a woman's life is the season of menses, the decades of possessing the (theoretical) ability to bear a child. Entering into this season is characterized by massive hormonal changes. It can be a difficult transition that often includes weight gain, breakouts, and titanic inner struggles. (Sorry.) Girls begin to really wrestle with the questions: *Who am I? What makes me valuable? Where do I fit in?*

Adolescence for most of us is hard.

This is the season you are either in or will be soon. Your menstruation marks the official beginning of puberty. Changes are going on inside your body that are mysterious and often uncomfortable. All those hormones being released can make it an emotionally volatile time. You are growing in every way a young woman can grow. Your body. Your soul. Your emotional capacity.

Did you know that as a teenager you actually feel things more strongly than adults do? It's true. You do. Joy, sorrow, loss, heartbreak—your emotions run deep. That's also why there's really no such thing as "puppy love." First love is intense. (That's one of the reasons you want to guard your heart!)

As your hormonal levels change and spike, it can be a challenge for your skin to keep up with it all. Also, boys are suddenly much more interesting. Passing glances or a simple brush against an arm can make your stomach lurch. In a good way. Relationships with other girls can feel much more difficult and their opinions seem much more weighty. Changeable too. Your friendships can become tricky. Adults can seem more stupid. Your mother more irritating. Your family more embarrassing.

It's normal.

Really.

It will pass.

It's also the season of life when you are more likely to take risks that later you wish you hadn't. Your biochemistry is changing. Some days you may just want to sit this "season" out, but you don't get to.

Well, maybe you can for an afternoon or even a week but not for long. It's actually one of the most fabulous times of your one wild and precious life.

How you feel, what you think, what you experience, and the choices you make in this season matter. Today. Now. Always. You matter. These may not feel like "wonder years" or anything close to the best time of your life, but it is still your life. Today will shape your tomorrow. Tomorrow you will remember yesterday.

In this season of your life, questions in your heart continue to be answered as you settle into your womanhood. Your monthly period may be regular or come only as a complete surprise, but these years make up the longest season of a woman's life. So keep tampons in your purse (or whatever your favorite feminine product of choice turns out to be).

How has puberty changed your life? How does it affect the way you see yourself?

The third season of a woman's life is known as perimenopause. Right now it feels like an eternity away. During this season, which lasts up to a decade, your feminine body will change in ways as dramatic as when you first entered into puberty.

The fourth season of a woman's life is called menopause. Menopausal women no longer have menstrual cycles, can no longer get pregnant, and don't need to worry about staining their pants. This season of life is a marvelous one too, with women stepping into a fuller expression of themselves. Creativity soars. Self-doubt and self-editing no longer hold the power they may have held when a woman was younger and less assured, and many women come to enjoy a previously unknown depth of self-appreciation.

There is a deep goodness to every season of life. Throughout every one, you are meant to grow in developing and offering your unique and God-given strength. You also get to enjoy being you— spring, summer, autumn, and winter!

life in a month

Okay, so there are four seasons to a woman's life. Now let's look at what is going on during the four weeks of our monthly cycle.

I'll just go ahead and admit that my favorite week of my menstrual cycle is the first one. I have energy and a positive attitude. I make plans to throw a party, join a club, exercise with gusto, and believe all the fabulous things God says about me in the Bible with more fervor than I did just a few days ago. Come on over and we'll bake a cake and then we'll take it to a homeless shelter. Yeah, baby.

My hormones are doing their life-bringing thing. I would like to believe that this version of myself is the truest me, but I'll still be me in three weeks when my friends begin to arrive for the party and I don't want them coming over to my house anymore. It's all me. The ups and downs, the highs and lows—and it's all you, too.

There are four weeks to a woman's cycle. Twenty-eight days. In the first week, estrogen is released and our ovaries begin work on an egg cell. Estrogen also helps to release other marvelous things in our brains like dopamine and serotonin. We are happier. Our energy level is at its highest. This is our "You go, girl!" week. (Sure, I'll run for class president!)

When the second week begins, things change. Estrogen levels off and then declines. We are still energetic, strong, and creative, just perhaps not so manic. Then ovulation occurs. Estrogen rises slightly and progesterone increases. The egg begins its journey down the fallopian tube. We are more peaceful inside and also perhaps more sexually alert. This is the week when holding fast to godly sexual boundaries may be more difficult.

(Can I just go ahead and say it? Keep your clothes on. Don't lie down while you are kissing. Rethink kissing. Okay, I'm not your mother, but I am a mother and sometimes my maternal instincts just take over. *Make good choices!*)

Then at the end of this week, our energy begins to lessen. Our emotions may become a bit conflicted.

> *The beauty, power, and wonder of your sexuality is too deep a subject for me to go into here. Others have written well on it, and I highly suggest you read more.* Every Young Woman's Battle *by Shannon Ethridge and Stephen Arterburn is a great resource!*

In the third week, if no egg was fertilized, our brains signal estrogen and progesterone to vacate the building. Emotions slide a little bit. Blood sugar levels slide too. We aren't feeling our confident selves as easily. For a few days, the empty space created by the departing hormones leaves many girls and women feeling empty inside as well.

Sometime during the fourth week, if we aren't pregnant, both estrogen and progesterone leave, and so does the endometrial lining that formed in our uterus to prepare a cozy place for an embryo. Our period begins. Chocolate is irresistible. Commercials make us weepy. We may cramp or ache or not even notice any physical discomfort, but emotionally, we may wish we could turn off our phone and disappear from our life for a couple of days. There is usually one or two days in this week for me when I don't believe I have any friends, but I don't care very much that I don't because I don't like anyone anyway. These are the days of the month to allow ourselves to slow down, take an afternoon nap, maybe journal. A bubble bath may sound mighty nice. If we have commitments (and we probably do), we pray extra hard and ask God for the strength and grace to fulfill them.

And then the crocus blooms. The daffodils make their happy appearance. Spring comes again and hope rises. The cycle begins again.

See, you're not crazy!

How are your hormones affecting you? Which week of your cycle are you in?

My menstrual cycles are ending, and I am just beginning to learn about them. Cycles have affected my mood for years, and just now I am learning that mood fluctuations are normal. I've felt crazy. Broken. Dismissible. Why didn't I chart them week by week before? (Dear one, please chart your cycle. Make notes in your calendar each month so you know where you are. It's so *helpful*.)

I have tried to live apart from my body, ignoring its cries for tending. I have tried to live apart from my emotions, ignoring their pleas for attention. It has not been a good choice. I've been living disconnected from my very self. I am my body just as much as I am my spirit, my soul, my emotions, my dreams, my desires, and my sense of humor. So are you. So honestly, right at this moment, I am not ignoring my very self. I will confess that I am low, tired, and my breasts feel heavy and sore. And because of what I've learned, I now know that this does not mean I am:

Depressed

Lost

Confused

Overwhelmed

Nuts

Making no headway

Moody

Forever stuck

It means my estrogen and progesterone are low. That's all. Isn't that a relief?

I am choosing to pray, asking Jesus to help me be kind to myself and to others, to allow myself to be tired and low. This is a normal and good part of being a woman. And yes, I do like the other weeks of the month much better. In my I-can-do-it-all week I want to write, speak, go for a run, experience more of the Holy Spirit, bring Jesus's healing, and paint a room. Today I don't want any of that. I want hot chocolate, bed, a movie, popcorn, and nobody to talk to me except to bring me pillows.

I am no expert on hormones, but there are experts available to us, and it is supremely important that we as girls and women honor ourselves and take the time to discover what is going on in our bodies and when. Hormones affect us emotionally, physically, and spiritually. For some of us the effect is painful and emotionally damaging. But we do not need to suffer by remaining alone in it. There is help on many fronts available to us. Talk to an adult friend, your mother, a teacher, a counselor, a doctor. Read a good book on the subject! If you feel the need, check into seeing a naturopath, a gynecologist, a hormone specialist.

And lean into God. Press in. The difficult days of each month can become a respite of hiding our hearts in our God, who always understands us and loves us endlessly. There is grace here. There is mercy here. For every one of us.

But let us begin here: do not curse yourself by cursing your body or your femininity. To be a girl is a glorious thing. Yes, we bear a suffering that guys do not know. This is not a reason to envy them or to curse ourselves. (By the way, you curse yourself when you say things like, "I hate my body; I hate my period; I hate hormones; I wish I were a guy.") Healing here begins with blessing:

I bless my body. I thank you, God, for making me a woman. I accept my body and my femininity as a gift. I bless these hormones inside me. I consecrate my feminine body to the Lord Jesus Christ; I consecrate my hormones to him. Jesus, come and bring grace and healing here. Speak peace to the storm within me just as you calmed the sea. Come and bless my femininity, and teach me to understand how you have made me and how to live with myself and the rhythms of my body.

What would you like to say to God about your monthly cycle? About your body?

Now, this was a brief glimpse at the internal setting of every girl's life. Time to turn our attention to the external landscape we all share. It might be more powerful than hormones, and I'll guarantee you it's having a mighty impact on many an unaware young woman.

the war around us

I recently read a story about a twelve-year-old girl in Ethiopia who had been abducted by men who planned to force her into marrying one of them. She'd been missing for a week when she was found. Terrified and bloody after having been severely beaten, the girl was being guarded by three lions that had come to her rescue and chased her captors away. Three man-eating lions that would normally attack people had miraculously saved her![2]

I love this story of another trinity coming to one in need. But after reading it, I learned that kidnapping and abusing girls in order to get them to marry is a common practice in Ethiopia. The United Nations estimates that more than 70 percent of marriages in Ethiopia come into being by abduction.

I'm not picking on Ethiopia here. Its history and current state of affairs mirror way too many other countries. The statistics on suffering in the world are mind numbing. But here is the story of one girl. I am amazed and grateful for this rescue and grieved for the millions of other girls who don't experience rescue themselves.

Most little girls at some point dream of living in a fairy tale. The big surprise when we grow up is not that the fairy tale was a myth but that it is far more dangerous than we thought. We do live in a fairy tale, but it often seems as if both the dragon and the wicked witch are winning. (Sometimes we feel that we are the dragon—that's the internal monthly battle, usually around week three.) But let me say with utmost seriousness, there is a battle going on around us every single moment of our waking and sleeping. The external landscape that we share is in the midst of a battle not only between good and evil but between life and death.

Things are not what they were meant to be. East of Eden, we have kept moving east and come all the way around, finding the garden utterly lost and cruelly unrecognizable. We were all born into this world. We came in gasping for air, and we are gasping still. It's a tough place to make a living, a hard place to make a life. Fire and ice. Beauty and terror. Pain and healing. Intertwined.

The good news is that Life wins out. Life has already won out. Love has won out. But the battlefield remains where we find ourselves, and the setting of the battle is a world that fiercely hates girls. God loves girls. Jesus loves girls. The Enemy, the Devil, has girls in his crosshairs.

Not a cheery thought but one necessary to face. Your life's journey runs through unfriendly terrain. You knew this already. The smoke from the heavenly engagement going on all around us affects our watery eyes and our labored breathing like smog. With mortars flying, aimed at our heart, we need to name it. So much of the sorrow in our lives finds its roots in misogyny.

the hatred of women

> Misogyny: a hatred of women. From Greek *misein*
> "to hate" + *gynē* "woman."[3]

The Greek philosopher Aristotle lived three hundred years before Christ and had a huge effect on the world as we know it. He believed that women exist as natural deformations or imperfect males.[4] He was not alone in his belief, and that belief has had an effect. That's the world you were born into. Misogyny colors our world, and the colors have bled into your life. Recognizing it helps us understand our life and navigate through it.

Misogyny is the hatred of women and everything female. It was birthed at the fall of man and has found its home not only in men but in women, too. It manifests itself in many different ways— from jokes to pornography to sex trafficking to the self-contempt a girl feels for her own body. Why is plastic surgery now common practice? Anorexia, bulimia, and bingeing all find their roots in self-loathing, in misogyny. The history of our world is rampant with damage, oppression, diminishment, contempt, and fear aimed at women and girls.

When Jesus came onto the scene, he turned misogyny on its head. A rabbi at that time wouldn't speak to a woman in public, not even his own wife (this is still true for Orthodox rabbis). Even today, an Orthodox Jewish man is forbidden to touch or be touched by any woman who is not his wife or a close family relation. Jesus didn't abide by those rules. During his ministry Jesus engaged with women many times. He spoke to them. He touched them. He taught them.

He esteemed them. He had women minister to him physically, touching him, washing his feet, anointing him with oil and with their tears. He had women disciples traveling with him, supporting him, learning from him, and "sitting at his feet." If we, the church, the body of Christ, had followed the example that Jesus set instead of the traditions of men held captive to sin and the fall, we would have a much higher history here.

But misogyny got into the church a long time ago. Many a Scripture-filled sermon has been preached throughout the centuries, advocating the suppression of women. We need to understand that the Bible records information and cultural practices that it does not support. The Bible describes in detail many acts of sin, but it does not endorse those acts. So it is with slavery—the Bible acknowledges it but does not endorse it. Yet slavery was supported from many pulpits in nineteenth-century America with sermons quoting Scripture. In the same way, Paul's words about women have too often been twisted to serve the oppression of women—far from his intention.

The good news is, it's changing. The truth also is that Christianity has done more to elevate the status of women than any other movement in history.

What do you believe Jesus feels about women and girls? Why?

In far too many cultures the status of women and girls is not changing at all. Yes, "we've come a long way, baby," but we've got a long way to go. Misogyny is fierce. It has come to us through people and governments and cultures and religions and nations. It comes through guys. It comes through women and girls.

Think back to the playground. Little girls can be catty, cruel, and competitive. Generally speaking, boys slug each other and five minutes later have made up and moved on. Girls are laying strategies for revenge. They wound with sophistication and deadly words.

Older girls compete with each other for the attention of guys. How many girls have sacrificed their best friend on the altar of "boyfriend"? Many girls are threatened by another girl's beauty, intelligence, and grace. We walk into a room and unconsciously size up all the other women. We quickly judge where we fit in the hierarchy of attraction (worth) without even being aware that we have done it. That behavior finds its roots in misogyny.

Remember, misogyny is hatred. Whether we are aware of it or not, when we hate other girls, we are hating ourselves, cooperating with the Enemy, and perpetuating grave damage. To hate, Jesus said, is to murder.

So of course misogyny can lead to physical acts of violence. From girls. From guys. The following tweet from Jimmy Carter brings this point home eloquently.

> The abuse of women and girls is the most pervasive
> and unaddressed human rights violation on earth.
> #violenceagainstwomen[5]

As is true for too many of you, my story includes sexual assault. One instance occurred when I was twenty. A guy followed me into a restaurant bathroom, locked the door behind him, and tried to force himself on me. I fought him. He ended up pinning me between the commode and the wall and pleasured himself. After climaxing, he released me and yelled, "Look what you made me do! Look what you made me do!" Then he left.

"Look what *you* made me do." He blamed me for his sin, his *hatred*. That is not an uncommon slant of reality.

But let us be careful not to fall into blaming or hating men. May it never be! Guys are to be esteemed. And so are girls. Masculinity is to be relished. Celebrated. Honored. Welcomed. And so is femininity. The sorrow guys reaped at the fall includes their separation from God and their separation from their *ezer*. God created Eve to be Adam's *ezer*, the Hebrew word in Genesis 2:18 that means his lifesaver, his counterpart, the one whom he literally cannot live and flourish without. God's intention was for men and women to support and complete each other, to be one in purpose, in mission, in love. But the fall came, and with it came division and sorrow beyond telling. Though much of the sorrow in our lives flows from human beings, people are not the enemy. Girls are not the enemy. Guys are not the enemy. Satan is the Enemy.

the true cause

Two children are sold into the human sex trade every minute, with nearly two million children forced into the worldwide sex trade each year.[6] Eighty percent of those trafficking victims are women and girls. And human trafficking is not a problem only in other countries—it is rampant in the United States as well. The United States is the number-one destination for sex tourism.[7]

Or how about this? Eighty percent of pornography that floods
the world is rated as "hard-core" porn.[8] When most of us think of
pornography, what comes to mind is "soft" porn. Hard-core pornography includes child pornography, sadomasochistic pornography,
insanely beyond-wicked pornography. All aimed to destroy the
hearts of every person coming near it.

The source of all this hatred and sorrow is not guys, not the
church, not even governments or systems of injustice. Scripture
makes it very clear that the source of evil is the Evil One himself:

> For our struggle is not against flesh and blood, but
> against the rulers, against the authorities, against the
> powers of this dark world and against the spiritual
> forces of evil in the heavenly realms. (Eph. 6:12)

Evil is rampant. And it is far too easy to blame people, organiza-
tions, the church, or political systems. But that will never change things
because that is a naive understanding of the world. Jesus called Satan
the prince of this world. Satan is the prince of darkness, whose sole aim
is to steal, kill, and destroy life in all its forms, and he has power here.
He has power here on earth, where and when the kingdom of God
is not being enforced or advanced. He is the source of the hatred of
women and girls, the hatred you have encountered. But let us remember: Jesus has won all victory through his crucifixion, resurrection, and
ascension. All authority in heaven and on earth has been given back to
him, where it rightly belongs. And then Jesus gave it to us.

I'll have more to say about this in a coming chapter. For now let
us acknowledge two things:

There is great evil in the world and much of it is directed at women.

The source of that evil is not guys or girls, but Satan.

If you will accept this, you can not only make leaps forward in understanding your life, but you can also find your way through the battle to the goodness God has for you and the goodness he wants to bring through you.

the way forward is love

When we hate girls, we hate ourselves. When we diminish the role of girls, we diminish ourselves. When we are jealous, envious, or slandering of other girls, we join the Enemy's assault on them. In doing those things we come into agreement with the Enemy by saying that what God has made is not good. It's time to stop doing that. The way to navigate the external battle begins with love. Not blaming, not finger pointing, but love.

Yes, the roles that have been dominated in the past by the female persuasion are the roles that are less valued by our society. Providing the backbone of our world are teachers, nurses, caregivers, professional assistants, you name it. Their work is diminished. The role of mother has been minimized as well.

But we do not overcome this subtle misogyny by trying to be guys any more than we overcome our feminine bodies by trying to "unsex ourselves," as Lady Macbeth attempted. Let us begin by celebrating femininity. The truth is that who we are as women, what we bring, and the role that is ours to play in the world and in the kingdom of God are of immeasurable worth and power.

The kingdom of God will not advance as it needs to advance without girls rising up and playing their role. Guys will not become the men they are meant to be without godly women and girls pouring into their lives. The transformation and healing of a guy requires the presence, strength, and mercy of women and girls. Girls will not become who they are meant to be without the strength, encouragement, and wisdom of other women and girls nurturing their lives. Yes, it will be hard. But that's because you are so vitally needed. Your valiant feminine heart is needed today in the lives of those you live with, go to school with, and love. The hour is late.

Girls are image bearers of God. Girls are coheirs with Christ. Girls are valued, worthy, powerful, and needed. There is a reason the Enemy fears girls and has poured his hatred onto our very existence. Let him be afraid, then. For "we are hard pressed on every side, but not crushed; perplexed, but not in despair; persecuted, but not abandoned; struck down, but not destroyed" (2 Cor. 4:8–9). We are more than conquerors through Christ who strengthens us, and we will not be overcome. God is our strength. Jesus is our defender. The Holy Spirit is our portion. And in the name of our God and Savior, we will choose to love him. We will choose to bow down in surrendered worship to our God. And by the power of Christ in us, we will choose to rise up and be women of God, bringing his kingdom in unyielding and merciful strength.

Have you experienced the hatred society has toward women and girls? If so, how? Think about ways girls as well as guys show that hatred.

Chapter Four

your mother, yourself

*If you want to understand any woman you must first
ask about her mother and then listen carefully.*

Anita Diamant, *The Red Tent*

Mark volunteered at an after-school program, tutoring high school students in English. Sister Janet, who was the driving force behind all aspects of the program, found out that Mark played the cello well, so she asked him to play for a school assembly.

Mark was not gung ho on the idea. He told Sister Janet that assemblies featuring classical music do not go well; they can get ugly. Sister Janet replied that their boys would never behave in an ugly way. Their "boys," by the way, were young men ages fifteen to seventeen, incarcerated in the Los Angeles Juvenile Detention Center, awaiting trial for crimes ranging from armed robbery to murder.

And she wanted Mark to play the cello.

Sister Janet was a force to be reckoned with, so she convinced Mark. The day of the assembly came, and Mark was escorted by a guard to the side room adjacent to the stage and told to wait. While he was waiting, he could hear the blasting sound of hip-hop music and the young men going crazy with happiness. He ventured a peek out the door and saw that the star of the show was a scantily clad young woman, musically challenged, banging on a tambourine.

Mark closed the door and slumped in his chair. In walked Sister Janet. Mark exclaimed, "This was a huge mistake! Listen to them out there! They're going crazy, and all that for a girl in a bikini!"

"There's a girl in a bikini out there?" Sister Janet asked, intrigued.

"It might as well be a bikini!" Mark whined.

"Have a little faith," Sister Janet urged.

The time came for the hip-hop group to leave. The guard opened the door for Mark and motioned for him to come onto the stage. As he walked across the stage, Mark tripped over his cello, earning him laughter.

Not anxious to play, he regaled the audience with interesting (to him) and boring (to them) facts about the cello until he just couldn't put it off any longer. "I'd like to play 'The Swan' for you. It's a song that always reminds me of my mother."

Mark began to play. The concrete floors, the bare walls, and the high ceilings made the room as resonant as a shower stall. The music was beautiful. But then he began to hear another sound, the sound of restlessness. Movement. Shuffling. *Oh great,* he thought, *they're bored already.* Risking a glance, he saw that the noise he heard was snuffling. The young men were wiping their runny noses on their sleeves. Tears flowed down their faces. Mark continued to play "The Swan" better than he had ever played it in his life. When he finished, it was to rousing applause.

"Now I'd like to play a sarabande by Bach." Mark again played well. After the smattering of applause, one young man yelled out from the back, "Play the one about mothers again!"

Oh.

It was not so much the beauty of the music that had moved the inmates but rather the invocation of motherhood. Mark played the song two more times and received a standing ovation. The young men booed the guard when he came to escort Mark off the stage.[1]

Mother.

In *The Pastor's Wife*, Sabina Wurmbrand shared that at night, in prison, when all is quiet, one word is called out in the darkness most often. It is a plea and a prayer all in one: "Mother."

On battlefields when the fighting is done and soldiers lie wounded and dying, one word is universally called out: "Mother!"

I called it out. I was twelve years old, and my brother had finally allowed me to ride his minibike. He gave me instructions on all things save one: how to stop. Our driveway was long and steep, and the trees bordering it hid the road. I flew down the driveway, increasing in speed as I went, sped straight across the road, smashed into the curb, and flew over the minibike, breaking my fall on the neighbor's wooden fence.

"Mom!" I cried.

She came running. She came with Mr. Next-Door Neighbor, and the two of them helped me limp to my room to my bed. A short while later, my mom came in to check on me, and her first words were, "You need to lose weight. You were really hard to carry because you are so heavy. It was embarrassing."

Mother.

It's a powerful word for a powerful woman who is influencing your life in all kinds of ways! Our mothers have blessed us and have wounded us.

Describe your relationship with your mother using only adjectives.

the power of a mother

Mothers comfort, teach, counsel, and guide. Well, they are meant to. Mothers are a source of wisdom, and they pass their wisdom, their way, their core beliefs on to their children.

Too often we diminish our mothers, both who they are and what they've done. We want to respect the weighty role they play in our lives. We want to honor our mothers (Eph. 6:2). We also need to be honest about them. Our moms affect us far more than most of us realize. How could it be otherwise?

Our mothers are made in the image of a powerful God. Remember, God said, "'Let us make mankind in our image....' In the image of God he created them; male and female he created them" (Gen. 1:26–27). That means that our feminine hearts find their root in the heart of our Creator God.

I am not questioning the gender of God or the fact that God is our heavenly Father. He most definitely, profoundly is. He is not our heavenly Parent. Father is masculine. But the Trinity—God the Father, God the Son, and God the Holy Spirit—does not have a gender but is the source of gender. There is the father heart of God. There is also the mother heart of God. I put some words earlier to what a mother is meant to do: teach, guide, impart wisdom, comfort. Does that sound like any member of the Trinity to you? The Holy Spirit maybe?

You carry so much dignity because you are a girl made in the image of God. So does your mother.

A great deal has been written on the impact a father has on his son or daughter. My husband and I have both talked about this ourselves in previous books (*Captivating, Wild at Heart, Fathered by God*). Every child enters the world with a core question, and the primary person they bring their heart's question to is their father. For boys the question is, *Do I have what it takes? Am I the real deal?* For girls it's, *Do you delight in me? Am I captivating?* But for both girls and boys, the deepest question is, *Do you love me?*

Because of the way God has created the universe, the father-child relationship is the deepest in our souls. The father bestows identity. This is who you are. This is your true name. How your father answered those questions for you—whether well or wrongly, cruelly or wonderfully—has helped to shape you into the young woman you are today.

How has your father answered these questions: Do you delight in me? Am I captivating? Do you love me? *What have you learned about your identity from your earthly father? Hold those beliefs up against the Word of God—how do they compare? Ask your heavenly Father to answer your heart's questions and to tell you who you truly are.*

Since our earthly fathers play such a huge role in shaping us, it can easily follow in our thinking that our mothers must play secondary roles, incidental roles. And that couldn't be further from the truth. The role of mother is massive.

The father bestows *identity*.

The mother bestows *self-worth*.

It was our mothers who answered our hearts' questions of: *Am I worth sacrificing for? Being inconvenienced for? Taking the time for? Loving? Do I have worth?*

We all have mothers. By virtue of the fact that you exist, you have a mother, and every mother's effect on her child is profound. Foundational. Emotional. Mental. Physical. Spiritual. Cellular. Your mother's effect on you began right after not your birth but your conception.

A baby being formed in the womb knows much, feels much, even hears much. It's documented that a baby in the womb is aware and that we actually remember at some deep level what was happening in our world while we were in there.

What happens in the womb sets the stage—sets the foundation for your life. When a mother is feeling happy, secure, and hopeful, the blood flow to her uterus opens up and fully nourishes the fetus. When a mother is feeling worried, anxious, or fearful, the blood vessels constrict and the flow of blood to the fetus is constricted. The developing baby does not get enough. That has an effect on every aspect of a fetus.

Much more than the mother's DNA is being imprinted on the developing baby. While still in the womb, the emotions of the mother translate into the baby. Questions are being answered in her tiny heart. *Is the world safe? Am I wanted? Am I secure? Will there be enough for me? Enough food? Enough emotional nourishment? Am I wanted? Rejoiced over? Panicked over? Am I coming into a dangerous living environment or a safe one?*

You see, a mother is a mother as soon as she conceives. All that is going on in her life during those nine months of gestation matters. It affects the child. It affected you.

> *What was going on in your mom's life while she was pregnant with you? If you don't know, ask her.*

Your mother is your primary role model. How she feels, what she thinks, and what she believes has a direct effect on you.

What our moms feel about their bodies plays a huge role in how we feel about our bodies. Our mothers' beliefs affect what we believe about ...

> What is possible in this life
> What we can attain, achieve, become
> What guys are like
> What God is like
> What friendships can be like
> What marriage can be like
> How we should care for ourselves

All that our mothers thought and felt was passed on to us. And we need to become aware of what that is. What does your mother believe? How does she treat herself and her needs? Do you know?

Whatever we learned or was passed into us from our mothers shapes us. Maybe what was passed on to you hasn't been so great, but it does not have the final say on who you will become. Jesus has come for you! You have been adopted into a new family and you have a new bloodline.

Mothers bestow our self-worth. And they have the ability to withhold it. Some mothers do withhold it intentionally, but more often any withholding is unintentional. *They cannot pass on what they do not possess.*

Mothers have the ability to withhold acceptance. Mothers can withhold love. Our mothers failed us when they—without wanting to or meaning to—passed on to us a low self-esteem. Low self-worth. Or when they based our self-worth on something—anything—other than the fact that we are here. We exist. We are!

God does not do that.

Our worth, our value, is not based on what we do, which life path we choose, or what we believe. Our worth is inherent in the fact that we are image bearers of the living God. Our worth is based on the fact that we are alive. We are human beings. Our worth is immeasurable.

Our worth as a girl or woman does not come to us when we believe in Jesus Christ as our Savior. It comes in our creation.

If we were not of value or of great worth, then the blood of goats and lambs, ox and bulls would have been enough to purchase humanity out of captivity. Back in the garden, the human race went into captivity and bondage, and the price to buy us back was so high that no ransom note was even given. But God knew and pursued us.

And he paid the ultimate necessary ransom to buy us out of captivity from sin and the Devil. We were hostages of such value that it took the blood of God himself to pay our price. You are of immeasurable value. You have a worth beyond counting.

a mother's labor

*My mother had a great deal of trouble with
me, but I think she enjoyed it.*

Mark Twain

The first two years of a person's life are *the* years in which the sense of self and self-worth is formed. And who is primarily responsible for that setting? Mom. Even if she is a full-time, out-of-the-home working mother who must return to her position when her infant is just two weeks old, it is not the caregiver who is forming her child's heart. It is the mom.

We do not live in a perfect world. I am a mother myself who has failed my children in innumerable ways. So in talking about our mothers, I'm not looking to cast blame. I'm looking for understanding and *healing*.

Were *you* satisfied? Once you were born, did you get enough? Food. Comfort. Safety. Love. Touch. Eye contact. Babies need their mother. They know her voice, her scent, and her face. Infants respond exponentially more to a woman's face and voice than to a man's.

Were you satisfied *as a child*? Were your basic needs for food, safety, and good touch met? Did you receive the attention you needed? Was the delight bestowed on you that you were meant to have? Were you celebrated simply because you existed as yourself?

Not getting enough feels the same as rejection. Not having your basic needs satisfied creates a deep sense of being unworthy and not enough, that something is wrong with you.

Are your basic needs being met now?

My mother smoked and drank while carrying me, back in the day when they all thought that was fine. (I know—can you believe it?) She was overwhelmed by her pregnancy with me. She was angry, scared, and, in her own words, "devastated" by my existence. I did not get enough while in the womb.

When I was born, it was into a family with an absent father and a mother who told my sisters that when they woke up, she would be gone. They sometimes woke up and ran into her bedroom to see if she was still there. My mother could not satisfy me. She did not have enough for me. Food. Time. Touch. Love. Attention. Care. Delight. Play. And it had an effect.

> *What about you? Did you get enough as a small child? Do you get enough now? What do you get enough of, and what don't you get enough of?*

A good mother fulfills four basic roles:

- She nurtures (provides food, safety, clothing, medicine, and all forms of personal and emotional support).
- She protects (from physical, emotional, or sexual harm or the threat of them). She intervenes on her children's behalf.

- She provides (educational, spiritual, and personal development opportunities).
- She prepares (initiates her children into adulthood and blesses them to become the full expression of their unique selves).

No one has a perfect mother. You don't. I didn't. Your mom didn't. My sons didn't. We have all been failed by our mothers to one degree or another. We all need healing in the places where we were missed or hurt. We need to forgive our mothers for the ways they failed us. We all need God to mother us in the places that need tending.

This is where the beauty of the mother heart of God comes in. God can meet our every need, heal our every wound, and bring his mercy to the places in our hearts that so desperately need it. We're going to pray at the end of this chapter and ask him to do just that.

> As a mother comforts her child, so will I comfort you. (Isa. 66:13)

welcoming Kacey into womanhood

Becky is a woman I love and respect. When her daughter Kacey began to mature, Becky and her husband, Jim, started to prepare Kacey with intention for all that was coming. Most of us didn't or won't receive this kind of initiation into womanhood, but I share her story because I want us to know what God can bring to us. I'll let Becky tell the story in her own words:[2]

We used the American Girls book entitled *The Care and Keeping of You* to begin the dialogue of what she could expect. We talked about her beauty in God's eyes, that she is a masterpiece created by our God. We went to a fun restaurant, where we ordered special drinks in a mug, but I brought a Styrofoam cup, too. We talked about how she is not "throw away" like Styrofoam, or serviceable like a mug; then I pulled out fine china and said she is like "fine china," priceless, hand painted, and carefully cared for…. We shopped for her first bras and made that very special! On the next outing, we talked about what she likes about her body and what she doesn't … that was great dialogue. One week we had pedicures and talked about the source of true beauty, using principles from *Captivating* to give her Jesus's true perspective. Lastly, we talked about beginning her monthly cycle, and I gave her a little bag with all the things she would need, just in case. The actual day she began her monthly cycle we made into a very special event with a date out to ice cream.

I just have to pause for a moment and say I know, I know—let the tears come for all that you wished you had and did not receive. I share Kacey's story not only to help you know what you were meant to have, but also to awaken your heart to the healing Jesus longs for you.

Throughout these couple of years, Jim began to date Kacey; the big event every year was taking her to the Daddy-Daughter dance held here locally. This past spring, at age fourteen, was the last dance they got to attend, and how perfect to have had her Calling Forth ceremony the same year, in this year of transition. Jim made this last dance very special by taking her shopping himself to find the "perfect" dress and accessories.

the calling forth ceremony

We prayed about what we were going to do for her Calling Forth ceremony. First of all, we kept it a complete surprise and also included family and friends who have played a key role in Kacey's life. Also, Jim had taken her shopping again one night, getting her a new dress (white) but not saying what it was for. As the evening began and after dedicating it to God in prayer, we told Kacey we were calling her out to be who God said she is.

Several weeks before this ceremony, Jim and I had asked her to write a paper, with no parameters, about what it means to be a Christian woman. We had her read to everyone what she had written; I believe this gave her ownership in all we were doing in her life.

Next, we showed the scene from *The Fellowship of the Ring* where Arwen rides with Frodo to the river. With her love of horses and her striking resemblance to Arwen, it really impacted Kacey's heart. Then our two boys, ages nine and seventeen, brought in Arwen's sword. Each of the boys spoke over Kacey and then handed me the sword. After them, I spoke over her life and what I see in her, and called her out as Arwen, as a warrior princess. We then passed the sword around, allowing each person to speak from their heart over Kacey's life. Lastly, the sword came to her dad, who then, after speaking, presented her with the sword.

We then explained that "Butterfly Kisses" was the song we played when she was dedicated to God as an infant, and began to play that song; about halfway through Jim asked her to dance. There was not a dry eye in the room. Then Jim took her on his lap and spoke about keeping herself pure; he pulled out a "promise ring" we had found especially for this evening. It has her birthstone in the middle, being supported or held up by my birthstone and Jim's. Inside the band of the ring it says "forever my daughter."

Then all gathered around Kacey, laying hands on her and anointing her for this next part of her life and sealing in her heart all that had been spoken. Some very dear friends presented her with a charm bracelet, where they each picked out a charm to give Kacey. The bracelet is incredibly meaningful to her. Throughout the whole evening a friend wrote down what each person said in a beautiful keepsake journal. Kacey goes back and reads it all the time and has added to it.

We have not done this parenting thing perfectly, but I believe that God has led us to give Kacey the tools, the affirmation of who she is in him, and the encouragement to live differently in a time that can be very hard for a teenage young woman. Just the other night Jim and I sat and held her together and prayed over her, building on all that we did in the Calling Forth ceremony.

I share this not because Kacey's parents did it all right, nor to suggest that this is the only model to follow. I share this because it is a beautiful picture of the love and intentionality you are meant to experience, the preparation you are supposed to receive as a young woman.

What do you believe it means to be a Christian woman? What feelings does Kacey's story evoke in your heart? In the Styrofoam verses fine china cup illustration Kacey's mom shared, what kind of cup do you feel you are? Have you been bra shopping yet? Get a good one. Or two. Yes to supportive. Yes to fitting. Yes to pretty.

Dear heart, reading this book is part of your initiation into womanhood. As you continue to read through the chapters and explore what it means to be you, consider the reality that this is all a part of Jesus calling you into the woman you are meant to be. You may not have your own ceremony. But Jesus is calling you forth.

I love the following scripture. I take it as a promise:

> But I have calmed and quieted my soul, like a weaned child with its mother; like a weaned child is my soul within me. (Ps. 131:2 ESV)

That can be true for us. Regardless of what we do or do not receive from our mothers, there is hope for us. There is healing. Nothing is out of reach for Jesus. *Weaned* means satisfied. *I am satisfied. I have had enough. All is well.* A weaned child is a satisfied child. Full. Content. Has enough. We can know that. In the deepest recesses of our hearts, we can know that. Dear ones, we *can* be satisfied. God put us in a world where we have him and we have one another.

Now to prayer. Take your time through this.

Holy Trinity, I invoke your healing presence now. Come and meet me here and now. I sanctify my memories and my imagination to you, God. I ask you to come and to reveal where I need healing, Jesus, and I ask you to heal me. Where do you want to come, God? Where do I need you to come? Is it while I was in the womb? Is it as a child, a little girl? Is it to every stage of my life? Come, Jesus. I ask you to come for me and to heal me in the deep places and unseen realms of my heart. I need you.

Come with your light and your love; come with your tender, strong, and merciful Presence and fill me here. In the name of Jesus, I bless my conception. God, you planned on me before the earth was made. I bless my development in my mother's womb. God, you were there. Come now beyond the bounds of time and minister to me, your precious one, as I was being formed in my inmost being, and speak your love and delight over me. I confess to you, God, and proclaim the truth that I have all I need. I am fully satisfied in you, Jesus, and I always will be. I am wanted, delighted in, and of immeasurable worth. You planned on me. You wanted me, and you still want me. Like a weaned child within me, my soul is satisfied in you, God. I break off any and all curses assigned to me, including all judgments against me passed on from my generational line. I am adopted into your family. The very blood of Jesus has purchased me, and I belong to you forever as your daughter. I claim this right here, in the womb. Together with you, Jesus, I bless my delivery. Come into that time and space, dear Jesus. Come into any and all trauma or fear that I may have experienced in that. I break off all assignments of fear or death that may have entered in through a traumatic birth in the name of Jesus Christ. Jesus, my healer, come into my need for nurture; come into the places that needed nurture from my mother. Show me where healing is needed here.

As you linger through this prayer, Jesus will show you memories and events and bring back feelings that you had. Were you satisfied as a child? Were your basic needs—for food, safety, and healthy touch—met? Did you receive the attention you needed? Was the delight bestowed on you that you were meant to have? Were you celebrated simply because you existed as yourself? Linger, and invite

Jesus here. As he reveals things to you, invite him in and ask him to heal. Is forgiveness needed here? Forgive. Are tears needed here? Allow those tears to come, but invite Jesus into those tears as you do. Ask for his healing. Ask him to nurture you in this very place. Linger, and then continue with the prayer.

Jesus, my healer, come into my need for protection; come into the places that needed protection offered to me by my mother. Show me where healing is needed here. And, Jesus, my healer, come into my need for preparation; come into the places that needed preparation from my mother and that need it today. Show me where healing is needed here. Father, thank you for my mom. I pray that I will honor her. I forgive my mother for every way that she fails me, unknowingly and knowingly. Please forgive me for the ways I have not honored, respected, or loved her. I bless her. I pray that you come for her and continue to mother her as well. Please come into my relationship with my mother. Bless it and help us to love each other wisely and well. Finally, Father God, in this moment I also repent of any and all hatred of girls and women that has taken root in my heart. Hatred of women is hatred of myself and not from you. I choose to love women, and I embrace my own womanhood. I thank you that I am a woman! I bless my femininity! I thank you for my life, and I choose life. I give my life fully to you now, Jesus, and I invite you to have your way in me. I love you, Jesus. Thank you for coming for me; keep coming for me. I pray all of this in your glorious and beautiful name, Jesus Christ. Amen.

Okay. That was good. It really was. Whether you felt anything or not, it was good.

A woman once told me that there are all kinds of ways God brings daughters into our lives, and I have found that to be true. Well, it is also true that there are all kinds of ways God brings us mothers, too. Spiritual mothers. Friends. Counselors. Christ himself.

If you don't have women you can say are mothering you these days, ask God to bring them. And as always, let God continue to mother you, to heal you. To guide, instruct, and comfort you. He's very good at it.

Chapter Five

be you. not them.

You never want
To know how much you weigh
You still have to squeeze into your jeans
But you're perfect to me
"Little Things" by One Direction

"Do you love your hips?"

The question threw me. Why in the name of all that is holy would I love my hips? The woman standing in front of me at the conference where I had just spoken was waiting for my answer. She repeated herself: "Do you love your hips? 'Cuz Jesus is not gonna heal you till you love your hips!"

Oy. Of all the things not to love about myself, I hadn't given much thought to my hips, but thinking of them in that moment, I could definitely say no, I did not love my hips.

The woman was telling me the truth. She was saying, God wants you to love and enjoy everything about yourself right now and embrace the truth that you are a beautiful woman regardless of your measurements. Until we can do that, we will not be moving forward. Or downward, as the case may be.

It's a difficult thing to stand in front of a mirror naked and tell yourself how marvelous your body is. It is contrary to every broken thing in a girl's or woman's soul and in this broken world. But I began to do it. Not so God would change my body, f-i-n-a-l-l-y. But so that I could begin to align the way I see myself with the way he does.

I began one evening in the bathtub by thanking God for my legs. I told myself I had fabulous legs. "I haven't been so kind to you, legs, but we've been through a lot together and you've brought me far. Thank you, legs. You're awesome."

And on like that. It became a practice. I stumbled a bit when I came to my arms. I still struggle with the arms. But okay, I'm going to do it right now. "Thank you, God, for these amazing arms. They work and hold things and open jars and steer wheels and pick up all kinds of things. Wow. I'm sorry for neglecting you, arms. You really are something else."

> *Go ahead and practice. Thank God for your body. Thank him for your legs, your arms, your feet, your hips, your face, your eyes, your teeth, your everything.*

beautiful now

One wonderful summer day last year, I was driving to the wedding of some dear friends' son. I was wearing a pretty dress that I particularly loved. Wanting to look extra nice, underneath the dress I was wearing a   suck-you-in-all-over-so-you-can't-breathe-but-your-torso-will-be-smooth torture device.

In my own mother's day, and in many days before her, the device was a lace-up girdle. My mother wore one regularly. Most women of her generation did, just as so many women of my generation wear the newfangled version. My mom once told me the story of her grandmother's sister immigrating to the United States from Germany. She was coming over from Europe on a ship (of course), and, wanting to look her best, she wore her corset. (You never know who you might meet! Jack! I'm flying!) She wore her corset the entire two weeks. She wore her corset as cinched as she could get it. She wore her corset so cinched that it prevented her from being able to go to the bathroom, and by the end of the journey to the New World, she was dead. Because of her corset. True story. Oh, sister, what price beauty?

Honestly, how many women have died in the quest to attain some just-out-of-reach level of beauty? It is a tragically high number.

So I was driving to Denver, wearing the hateful undergarment, when it became so painful I could barely breathe. It was digging into my ribs. I guess it's made for wearing while you are standing up, not sitting down for an hour behind a wheel. Thankfully, I was able to hoist my skirt up and get a hand underneath and pull the girdle thingy away from my body. But seriously, it took all my strength. I made a fist and let it press against that. Driving with one hand, at least I could breathe. But I needed to keep switching hands every few minutes because the thing was so unbelievably strong and tight.

And by the way, it was a size larger than I was currently wearing. So it's not that I had on the wrong size. It's that the things are supposed to strangle your body into a size or two smaller. Seriously now, why do we feel the need to do this to ourselves? What is so horrific about bumps? Please tell me. We are killing ourselves figuratively and literally to fit into the world's definition of what we are supposed to be.

My mother used to say, "Beauty before pain!"—meaning, being beautiful is more important than not feeling terrible. High heels with our toes pinched into the pointy tip. Spanx. Waxing. Trimming. Starving. Plucking. P-a-y-i-n-g.

One of the assignments my mother gave me as the youngest daughter in my family was to pluck the coarse black hairs protruding from her chin when she was no longer able to see them or care. She made me promise not to leave her to this indignity. She was a nurse who often tended older women, and she grieved for those whose personal grooming was ignored. My mom was well acquainted with those pesky little black hairs. She had a magnifying mirror in which she would look to peruse and destroy any interlopers. Pluck! Pluck! Pluck!

At about the age of thirty, I made the mistake of looking at myself in her well-lit magnifying mirror. WHAAAAT? Oh my gosh! Why did no one tell me I had a beard? Where are the tweezers? I was horrified. Are you kidding me? What was unseen to the mere human eye, or just by looking in a regular mirror—even up close—was magnified to werewolf proportions in my mother's mirror.

Pluck. Pluck. Pluck.

be you. not them.   89

My mom gave me her mirror. I was hooked. When it broke, I bought myself a new one. A bigger one. A better-lit one.

My husband is urging me to throw the thing away. I have told him that throwing it away is in my future. But I'm not ready yet. Maybe I'll be ready when I've attained a zit-free, hair-free status. Or better, maybe I'll throw it away when my soul more fully embraces the truth of what God says about me. God has been inviting me to throw the magnifying mirror away and be free, free from gazing at my multiple imperfections in my face and in my soul and instead to believe the reflection he is showing me. *Honestly, the only reflection that really matters is the reflection we see in his loving and joyous eyes.* What does he see? What does he say? He says we are beautiful *now*.

> *Do you believe you are beautiful now? What helps you believe that? What gets in the way? Ask God to help you believe what he says about the physical you. By faith, bless your body. Out loud. Right now. Do it often!*

embraceable you

Our bodies are God's gift to us through which we experience the world. Our five senses are windows that illuminate our lives. We need to care for every part of ourselves, nourishing and guarding our hearts, our souls, and our bodies.

In chapter 1, I said we need to be nice to our hearts. Well, we need to be nice to our bodies, too. We need to pay attention to when we are hungry and feed our bodies nourishing food. We need to notice when we are tired, not ignore the signals, and give ourselves rest. We want to strengthen our bodies with exercise and movement. We want to say nice things to ourselves about our bodies.

Got you on the last sentence, didn't I?

Just last night, I caught myself telling myself that my body is ugly. Oy. Not again. I repented. I said out loud, "No. My body is not ugly. I love my body. I am beautiful."

That's how it works. I caught myself being mean, so I stopped. I chose instead to say to myself what God says about me, and honestly, it has a powerful, life-bringing effect.

What do you tell yourself about your body? How do you feel about it? What would you like to change? Even now, take a moment and tell yourself kind things about your body even if those words feel untrue.

The season of growth you find yourself in may make you uncomfortable with how your body is or isn't changing. We grow. We lose weight. We gain weight. Our hormones go nuts. Our breasts get larger ... or they don't. My friend Bethany was embarrassed about her breasts. Actually, most women I know are now or have been ashamed by or disappointed with their breasts. I have been. In her pre-bra elementary school days, Bethany put Band-Aids over her nipples because she was ashamed of them. Many older girls try to enhance their breast size by stuffing their bras or wearing padded ones. The ten-year-old daughter of a friend of mine was having a sleepover when she came out of her bedroom and her mother saw toilet paper poking out from her top. I tried that too. It doesn't work well. Toilet paper is scratchy and poky and lumpy. Another friend of mine was embarrassed about how large her breasts were, so she would squeeze them into a smaller size. (Many adult women continue to feel distraught over the size of their breasts and go the route of surgery for an enhancement or a reduction.)

Exploring what we would look like with a larger bra cup is part of growing up. That is simply normal curiosity. But the shame part? Shame and embarrassment over your body does not have to be part of your story at any age.

There's no shame in Christ, friends. No shame. You are you. Unique. Marvelous. Beautiful. Quirky. And imperfect. In Christ, as with all loved ones, you don't need to hide who you are. You actually aren't meant to hide at all.

In junior high, I would hide my face behind my hair. I wore it long and straight and tried to have only my nose poke out. That's because my cheeks were covered with pimples. Not little whiteheads, but deep, red, large blemishes.

During puberty our skin rebels. For some of us, the rebellion is more like a violent coup. Sweetheart, you are not alone, and this is not the end of your story. It's hard and painful and it will pass. When we look in the mirror, we see the flaws. We see our shortcomings. What is glaringly ugly to us is barely noticeable to others. You are not your skin. But your skin will get better. This is tough, but it will pass.

No, really. Still, please care for yourself. Speak words of truth. There is power in saying it out loud: "I am pretty." "I am loved." "God says I'm lovely." Speak the truth and use a gentle cleanser, and if you need it, ask to see your doctor. There are medicinal treatments available now that may make you feel like it's worse in the short run but in the very near future will clear up your acne amazingly.

You are worth caring for. Body and soul. You are worth accepting. You are worth embracing.

It can be hard to be happy with how God made you at any particular time but especially in the teen years. Those who are tall want to be short. Those who are short want to be tall. Those with curly hair long for straight, and those with straight hair want more body to it. We feel we are too flat or too curvy, too little or too big, not enough or too much. And it doesn't feel good.

Theodore Roosevelt said, "Comparison is the thief of joy." He's right. It's so easy in this world to compare ourselves to others. When we do that, we simply do not measure up. We tend to compare our worst with another girl's best, and that makes us feel terrible. Feeling despair over who we are or what we look like causes us to reject ourselves.

And that is the opposite of what Christ does.

He says you are just right, right now. His invitation to you in this very moment is to accept your body, accept your personality, accept all of yourself. Just as you are. He made you *you*. He's not waiting for you to become something other than who you are in order to be loved by him. He loves you now. He accepts you now. He not only accepts you, but he embraces you and he wants you to embrace yourself as well.

Now, I know that embracing ourselves is a stretch for most of us, but please know that embracing ourselves has nothing to do with arrogance or settling for a lower version of who we are. Embracing ourselves has everything to do with embracing the goodness of God's creative work in us. It means trusting God, believing that all he has made is glorious and good. And that includes us. You are the only one who can be you. The world, the kingdom of God, and all those around you need you to embrace who you are created to be as you become more fully your true self.

God wants you to be you. He wants you to offer you. He wants you to embrace you. So, who are you?

A good way to discover what makes you uniquely yourself is to answer the question, "What do I want?" Or this one: "If I could do anything at all and know that it would go smashingly well, what would I do?"

dream a little

How do you feel about desire? Does it feel like a bad thing? No, desire is really that core place in our hearts where God speaks. Years ago, in a small group I was in, we were invited to dream. We were given paper and told to write down what we wanted. To write a long list. Not to edit it. Nothing was too small or large to write down. My list turned out to be two pages long and had things on it as varied as the garden I wanted to nurture, the size I wanted to wear, the hope to ride horses with my husband, the healing I longed for a few dear ones to experience, and the wedding of a single friend I wanted to dance at.

I found that list a few years ago, and to my astonishment every single item had come true. It had happened! I needed to make a new list! I have!

God dreams big. And he invites us to dream big with him. God has planted dreams and desires in each one of our hearts, and they are unique to us. Opening up our spirits, our minds, our hearts, our imaginations to what we would really like—to even the possibility of wanting—allows the Holy Spirit to awaken parts of ourselves that are in such a deep sleep no dreams are happening.

God is a Dreamer. He has dreams of you and for you.

When we dream with God, we don't want to run to thinking, *How can I make this happen?* Dreaming with God isn't about how. It's about what. If anything could happen, then what would I love to see happen in my life? What would I love to see happen in the lives of those I love?

This book is about *your* heart. This moment is about your dreams and your desires that contribute to the unique, marvelous young woman you are. The point is not so much being able to name the desire as it is to allow God to access the places in your heart where dreams and desires are planted. God speaks to you there. About himself. About you.

It's okay to want, and it's okay to want *more*. Wanting more has nothing to do with being unsatisfied or lacking in your present reality. It's being open to the more that God wants to bring to you in your own life. The possibilities for you are limitless! They are. Yes, they are. Maybe not for tomorrow but for your *life*.

What is pushing it with God? What can't he do? What is too hard for him to accomplish in your relationships, your achievements, your creativity, in the fullness of the expression of who you are? We want to continue to grow all our lives. We never want to stop. Yes, we rest. But a heart alive is a heart that is awake and curious and pressing in for more.

What do you really want?

Four out of five Americans say they don't have any dreams, and we can imagine why. Life can suck the dreaming right out of you. The living God wants to pour those dreams back in. Sixteen percent of Americans say they do have dreams, but they don't write them down. Four percent have dreams and desires and write them down, but less than 1 percent review and update them on a regular basis.[1]

It is the people who allow themselves to dream, who own their dreams, and who write them down and look at them periodically whose life dreams are coming true. (They also earn nine times more money over their lifetime than people who don't. Think of what you could do with that! What good could you bring? What ministry could you support?)

I encourage you to risk dreaming and writing your dreams down. Once you get started, you'll find there are things you want. And if you can't get started, another approach is simply to begin listing the things you like. What do you like? From the fragrance of lilacs to a comforter before a fire to laughing with friends, it's nourishing simply to become aware of what you enjoy and to write it down.

It's good to sit with God in the quiet and ask him, *What do I want?* And ask him, *What do you want for me?*

Awakening and owning the dreams that God has placed in our hearts isn't about getting stuff or attaining something. It's about embracing who we are and who he has created us to be. In him. He is our dream come true and the one true love of our life. But we can't love him with our whole hearts when our hearts are asleep. To love Jesus means to risk coming awake, to risk wanting and desiring.

Jesus, come. Guide me. Holy Spirit, fill me. Dream with me and in me. Help me to unlock the desires you have planted in my heart and to write them down. Help me to dream big.

> *Ask yourself: What would I love to do? What would I love to experience or create or offer? What do I want to be really good at? What do I want with God? What does God want with me? What do I want to be known for?*

Dream. You have permission to dream. And besides, if you don't have a dream, how can you have a dream come true?

Chapter Six

beauty secrets

*Promise me you'll always remember: you're braver than you believe,
and stronger than you seem, and smarter than you think.*

A. A. Milne

*How beautiful you are, my darling! ... Your
eyes behind your veil are doves.*

Song of Solomon 4:1

I watched a YouTube video last week to learn how to do spring makeup. Do you know how much makeup you need to apply so you don't look like you are wearing any makeup? Layers. Still, I want to look "springy," so I tried. I tried the light, airy, barely there foundation. On the third day my face broke out in a riot of red. My skin rejected it. Dang. I just wanted to look pretty and it backfired. Beauty is tricky.

Beauty is also powerful. It may just be the most powerful thing on earth. Beauty has been extolled and worshipped and kept just out of reach for most of us. What the world defines as "beautiful" changes over time and cultures. Currently, the physical standards of beauty held up in the media as the goal are actually out of reach for 98 percent of the population.

"This is what is beautiful," we are told. "Look like this! Try to be this! You never will be able to, but please keep trying because we are making a lot of money out of your continued failed attempts."

It can make you feel horrid. I think it's meant to. I think it's actually wicked.

We are not supposed to measure ourselves by the world's mirror. There is not lasting life there.

While much of the world is suffering for a lack of food, the diet industry is making billions. B.i.l.l.i.o.n.s. Programs and products promising weight loss cures and lean bodies deliver only a taste of hope. They are tastes that don't last because the programs don't work. But we don't know that. We blame ourselves, and our inner agony turns into self-contempt.

We lose hope. Then we hear of something new and, what the heck, let's give that a try. I know. I've tried almost all of them. They don't work because we are trying to squeeze ourselves into beauty from the outside. True beauty is an inside-out process. It's internal first. *It's about your heart.*

> *Are there programs, regimes, techniques that you have tried*
> *for beautifying yourself that haven't worked?*

The desire to be beautiful comes from our heart and is a good and holy desire. Remember, you are made in the image of God! God is nothing if not absolutely gorgeous. Just look at the splendor of creation! The works of an artist tell you something about themselves. Look around. God is stunning.

Of course we want to be beautiful too. The truth is, you actually are.

Every woman has a beauty unique unto herself. I have seen beauty in virtually every woman I have ever met regardless of skin type, body shape, age, hair color, teeth whiteness, or number on the scale. Every woman is beautiful. You are beautiful. I am beautiful. Though I have recognized it in other women for as long as I can remember, I have only begun to see it in myself. Yes, I believe I am beautiful. Some days. Well, some moments.

May God help us all to believe it more deeply and more often. In the places where we don't believe it, we continue to shame ourselves. And shame will never lead us into the life we want to live.

Audrey Hepburn, an iconic beauty, once said, "The beauty of a woman is not in a facial mode, but the true beauty of a woman is reflected in her soul." And quoting Sam Levenson she said, "'For beautiful eyes, look for the good in others; for beautiful lips, speak only words of kindness; and for poise, walk with the knowledge that you are never alone.'"

Dear heart, you are never alone. You are seen and known and loved. First John 4:10 says, "This is love: not that we loved God, but that he loved us and sent his Son as an atoning sacrifice for our sins." Dear heart, you are loved.

Beauty Secret #1: A woman becomes truly
beautiful when she knows she is loved.

reaching for control

In the tenth grade I went on a dare with my sister to see who could go the longest without eating anything. As we both had a few pounds to lose, my mother encouraged the competition. I was really happy when nearing the end of day three, my sister called to tell me to go ahead and eat. She had caved. Hoorah!

Going a day or two without eating was my modus operandi for many years. Just to keep within the normal weight range. I never crossed over into anorexia or bulimia. My obsession with food took (takes) the form of bingeing but without the purging.

I used to kind of envy women who engaged in bulimia. At least they looked good! I envied them a little, that is, until I got to really know a girl who battled it. It was horrible. The lengths she went to make herself purge were painful and extreme. Her toilet was her closest friend. She was damaging her body and ravaging her soul. Tormented, she was obsessed with food. Trying desperately to control her world, she found that bulimia was controlling her. She was motivated by fear and a deep self-loathing that no physical purging could exorcise.

I know many young women who have struggled with anorexia as well. Except in extreme cases, these girls can look pretty good too. From a distance. But they are on a rigid regime of self-deprivation and intense exercise fueled by fear and self-hatred. They aren't free. They are slaves to calories and nutrition labels. Their efforts to control their lives turn on them viciously. Their periods stop, they are cold all the time, and the damage to their internal organs can become irrevocable. One gal I love was nicknamed Skelly because she looked like a walking skeleton. But not to herself. What she saw when she looked in the mirror was quite different.

Honestly, the ability to look in a mirror and see what everyone else sees is rare. We see our flaws. They might as well be blinking in neon orange. *We can't see past what other people do not even notice.*

Sweetheart, if you struggle with an eating disorder, know that you are not alone. To become free of it—free from the desperate need to control your food, free from obsessing over it, free from the emotional suffering—you need help. This battle is not one you will be able to fight on your own. To be free from this horrible struggle you are enduring, please confess it to your parents, your pastor, a teacher, or a counselor. Help is available. You can be free. This overwhelming struggle is keeping you from living the life you are meant to live and offering what you are meant to offer. We need *you*.

Your beauty is under siege. It is being harassed and taunted and mocked because it matters. You matter. The Enemy of your soul attacks the core of your heart by attacking your beauty in order to pin your heart down and keep you from being the young woman you truly are. You are a powerful child of God. Your beauty is powerful. As an image bearer of the living God, you possess a beauty that is deep and true and core to your soul. It manifests itself on the outside but is first and foremost an inward quality. It blooms in the soil of confidence, assurance, and a happy heart.

Beauty Secret #2: We are at our most outwardly beautiful when we aren't obsessing over our outward beauty.

The apostle Peter said, "Your beauty should not come from outward adornment, such as elaborate hairstyles and the wearing of gold jewelry or fine clothes. Rather, it should be that of your inner self, the unfading beauty of a gentle and quiet spirit, which is of great worth in God's sight" (1 Pet. 3:3–4).

Peter was not saying, "Don't fix your hair or wear jewelry." He wasn't saying, "Only wear frumpy, out-of-style clothes." No! He was saying, "Don't fixate on your outward appearance, but center your attention on your heart."

"A gentle and quiet spirit" does not refer to a woman who barely talks above a whisper and never gets angry. "A gentle and quiet spirit" speaks of a heart that is filled with faith. Not doubt. Not fear. Not anxiety. Faith. Beauty flows from the heart of a young woman who is resting in the truth that she is loved, seen, known, wanted, and lovely to her heavenly Father. Right now. That young woman lives with self-confidence. And self-confidence is beautiful.

You can have that. You are a true beauty. Really. And it is right and good that you want to be because you are a reflection of Beauty Himself.

Ask God to show you your beauty.

courage

It takes courage to grow up and become who you really are.

e. e. cummings

Believing that you are beautiful can feel risky. To risk anything requires that we possess the courage to risk it. Jesus said, "In this world you will have trouble. But take heart! I have overcome the world" (John 16:33). Some versions translate "take heart" as "be of good courage." Courage is from the Old French word *cor,* meaning "heart." Take heart. Have courage. "Because of me," Jesus said, "you can do this."

Jesus knows that continuing to become free to be ourselves will take courage! There is a reason we shrink back from our hearts, from love, from our dreams, from our vulnerability. But, friend, the days of shrinking back need to be over. With mercy in his eyes, God calls us to be women of courage:

> Have I not commanded you? Be strong and coura-
> geous. Do not be afraid; do not be discouraged, for
> the LORD your God will be with you wherever you
> go. (Josh. 1:9)

> Do not let your hearts be troubled and do not be
> afraid. (John 14:27)

> Do not give way to fear. (1 Pet. 3:6)

We live in a world filled with beauty and wonder, adventure and laughter, but also too often filled with difficulty, fear, danger, and pain. Courage is the quality of spirit that enables one to face danger, pain, difficulty, or fear with confidence. We can have confidence! Not based on our own ability to manage life but based on the faithfulness of Jesus.

Confidence is from the Latin words *con* and *fide*, which mean "with faith." Our confidence rests in the strength and goodness of God. Living a life of courage is not about striving to become something or someone else. It is resting by faith in the God who says, "I have called you, and I will do it!" (see 1 Thess. 5:24).

Receiving the life of God is the only way for us to live the life we all so long to live. On our own, we simply can't pull this life off. I can find my way to the freeway, but I can't find my way to freedom. I can barely pull off an afternoon; forget about a lifetime. So what is the biggest secret to living with courage and freedom and becoming who God created you to be? To becoming deeply, truly beautiful? I'll tell you.

beauty secret #3

The biggest secret is you can't. *You* can't. But Jesus can. *Christ in you can.* He is the secret! God is beautiful and God is fearless. Jesus, who died on the cross for you, entered into the worst nightmare imaginable and demanded that Satan hand over the keys to hell. Jesus rose triumphantly and is seated at the right hand of God. This same Jesus:

> Calmed the storm and walked on the water
> Healed the leper and fed the thousands
> Gave sight to the blind, hearing to the deaf, and life
>   to the dead
> Cleared the temple and received the children
> Rebuked the Pharisees, forgave sinners, and cast
>   out demons

And he is still doing it. Jesus is alive today and living his beautiful, bold, glorious life through you. Remember, "I have been crucified with Christ and I no longer live, but Christ lives in me" (Gal. 2:20). Paul says the whole mystery of the gospel comes down to this: "Christ in you, the hope of glory" (Col. 1:27).

Christ is your life and your breath and your hope and your courage. In him you live and breathe and have your being. And apart from him, you can do nothing (John 15:5). But once you have accepted Jesus as your Lord and Savior, received his death in your place, received his forgiveness for your sins, and invited him to take his rightful place and rule your heart, you will never be apart from Christ again.

You are in the palm of his hand, and nothing can take you out. That's the secret of being truly beautiful! We increasingly lean on Jesus, calling on him to live his life through us. And as he does, we are transformed into the very image of God.

> Not merely in the words you say,
> Not only in your deeds confessed,
> But in a most unconscious way
> Is Christ expressed.
>
> Is it a beatific smile?
> A holy light upon your brow?
> Oh no! I felt his presence
> when you laughed just now.
>
> To me, 'twas not the truth you taught,
> To you so clear, to me still dim,

But when you came you brought
a sense of him.

And from your eyes he beckons me
And from your heart his love is shed,
Til I lose sight of you and see
The Christ instead.[1]

As this poem so eloquently expresses, Jesus is inviting us to relax into the beauty he has bestowed upon us and cease striving to attain a level of smooth perfection that looks wonderful on a doll or on a magazine cover but is not attainable in the living, breathing realm of humanity. God does not tell us that the goal is perfection. There, I said it. Now we can improve. We can grow. We can become more loving, more grace filled, more merciful, more strong, more wise. We are no longer bound to sin, slaves to its din of temptation. We are still going to sin. But we don't have to. Because of Jesus.

The more we know Jesus as he really is, the more we love him. The more we love him, the more our lives are transformed and the more beautiful we become. *The more his we become, the more ourselves we become.*

Be brave.

Veronica Roth, *Divergent*

To continue on the journey of becoming free to be ourselves, free to become even more beautiful, we need him to strengthen us

when we are too weak to believe. We need him to breathe his fiery
love into the chambers within that are frozen by fear. We need him
to hold our hope and tend our hearts and tell us once again who we
are. We cànnot do this alone.

Thank goodness we are not alone.

> God is within her, she will not fall;
> God will help her at break of day.
> (Ps. 46:5)

immeasurable

Some things can be measured scientifically. Weight. Height. Age.
The fact that infants respond more to a girl's smile than to a guy's. All
kinds of things can be measured.

But how do you measure the fragrance of a girl? The beauty
of a comforting touch? The joy of a smile? The warmth of an
embrace? Tears of empathy? Eyes that welcome, accept, and love?
How can you quantify the sound of a laugh that makes you feel
to your bones that all is right in the world? How can you possibly
dissect beauty?

That would be like pinning a dead butterfly to a board. What
then would you know of the wonder of its flight or what is drawn
from the heart while watching its aerial dance?

Outward beauty is a thing that can be measured only when
we accept the standards of measurement. Youth passes, so youthful
beauty fades. There are wrinkles around my eyes now. Laugh lines
are earned! Gravity takes its toll, but who wants to live in a cage,

fearful of the ravages of time? Life is to be lived! Beauty, true beauty, increases. It increases over time as it is offered, shared, and spent on others. It increases as our eyes open to the beauty surrounding us in God's creation and in each and every one of his image bearers. It grows as Jesus captures more of our hearts with his own and we are transformed into his very likeness. It expands as we believe we are who he says we are: his very beloved.

How can you measure the beauty of a sunset? Of a child laughing? Of the living God? Of you?

God says you are beautiful. More beautiful than any other thing in all creation. And, well, he ought to know.

Okay, you want more tangible beauty tips? Here they are! Be happy. Be kind. Discover what you love to do and do it! Try new things! Be creative in some way! Move your body! Take care of your one and only skin. Cleanse gently. Be generous with moisturizer and sunscreen. Use natural products as much as possible. Drink plenty of water, get enough sleep, and try to eat healthy foods 80 percent of the time! And most importantly, choose to believe the truth that you are loved right now.

Love is always the highest goal. Love of God, love of others, and love of ourselves. We don't want to live in spite of ourselves, but we want to embrace ourselves, owning the multifaceted mysterious women we are and the unique way we bring Jesus to the world.

You are the only you there has ever been or ever will be. God made you you on purpose. Now. For a reason.

The world does not need yet another young woman who despises the lovely creation that she is. God does not long for another girl who rejects herself and, by extension, him. The world needs a young woman who is thankful for how God has made her, trusts that he is transforming her, and actually enjoys who she is. It's a good thing to like who you are. God likes you! We get to like ourselves too! When you like yourself, you are free to enjoy others, and in your presence people experience an invitation to become and enjoy who they truly are as well.

Life begets life. Joy begets joy. Beauty begets beauty.

receiving a vision of yourself

A few years ago, I was at church and in a very low place. I felt hideously ugly. I was telling myself that I looked like Jabba the Hutt. (Not very nice words to say to oneself.) Kneeling in prayer, I asked God, "How do you see me?" In my sanctified imagination, I immediately saw a woman kneeling. The sun filtering through the window framed her in a golden beam of light. She was wearing a lovely fitted white satin dress. Her hair was softly yet ornately done up with seed pearls in it. She was beautiful.

He saw me then as beautiful. He sees me now as beautiful.

When God looks at his daughter—me, you, any beloved one—he does not view her through the veil of her sin, the shroud of her failures, or the canopy of her past. When God looks at us, he sees us through the blood of Jesus. When God looks at you, he sees the righteousness of Jesus Christ. You are a spotless, pure, stunning bride. Oh, how we need to see ourselves as he does! Both who we are in this moment and the woman he is forming in us.

We need to ask God for a more radiant picture of
Him and a more brilliant picture of ourselves.

Graham Cooke

Who do you think you are? Who are you on the road to becoming? Do you have a vision of who you could become? How does God see you? What is his vision of who you are to become? Ask him that question. And then wait for his answer.

Having a vision of who you are becoming informs your present. We live today knowing who we are going to be tomorrow. Knowing who you are becoming puts hope in your heart and a spring in your step. The key is to choose to believe we are who God says we are. And then rest in the knowledge that God is the One responsible for our transformation. We lean into him. We will fail. He will not.

So ask him, *How do you see me, God? Please give me your vision of the woman I am to become.* And then write it down. Write down what you hear from God or merely what, by faith, you choose to believe is becoming true for you because you want it to be!

Once you do, go ahead and risk. Embrace the vision, accept it, believe it, and move toward it.

Ask God for his vision of who you are becoming. Write down what you want to be true.

We need to risk believing that what God has said about us is *true*.

We must risk being more beautiful, more powerful, more loved, more loving, more involved, more connected, more glorious, and more gifted than we thought we ever could be.

We must risk believing we are worth loving, fighting for, protecting, and cherishing. God has revealed the truth to us through his Word. You want to know what he thinks about you? Open up the Bible. Camp out in Ephesians 1 for a few months! God has revealed himself to us through his Son, Jesus Christ. Want to know what God is like? Look at Jesus. He is the face of God. (To know what Jesus is really like, read *Beautiful Outlaw*. I cannot recommend it highly enough!)

God has revealed both himself to us and ourselves to us. Now we must flex our muscles of faith and choose to believe him in the moments when we are experiencing it and when we are not.

You are loved. You are beautiful. And that's not a secret.

Be who God meant you to be and you will set the world on fire.

Catherine of Sienna

Chapter Seven

stumbling into freedom

Resisting is worth doing.
Veronica Roth, *Four: The Transfer*

John and I went to the zoo recently. I loved seeing live-and-in-person lions, snow leopards, giraffes, elephants, gorillas, piranhas, and glow-in-the-dark tree frogs. There was an amazing section of oriental birds decorated more intricately than geishas. I've never seen anything like them before. There were flamingos, California condors, and two bald eagles enclosed in a habitat with high nets. There was a turtle that lives at the bottom of lakes that was the ugliest thing I have ever seen. Crazy. Wonderful.

Later that same day, we went for a hike in the hills. It was a glorious, sunny day with a strong breeze blowing. Coming back down, we stopped at the cry of a hawk and looked up to see three of them: soaring, diving so fast, then up, up, up. Chasing each other, then hovering and still—they flew with the aerial gymnastics of angels.

They were awesome. They were *free*.

I felt bad for the wild birds I had just seen in captivity. I understand zoos and I am not anti-zoo, but living in cages is not what those birds were created for. They are not living their best life now! At the zoo it had been wonderful to see bald eagles up so close. How huge they are! But I've seen bald eagles eating fish on the banks of the Snake River. I've seen them looking out over their domain from the protected heights of a stately pine, and I've seen them battling golden eagles over their nests.

Freedom is better than captivity.

So why in heaven's name would anyone choose captivity? Why do we live so long in the bondage we find ourselves in? There's a passage in Isaiah that I'd like every girl to hear:

> Shake off your dust;
>> rise up, sit enthroned, Jerusalem.
> Free yourself from the chains on your neck,
>> Daughter Zion, now a captive. (Isa.
> 52:2)

Free yourself? Isn't it Jesus who sets us free? Indeed he does; he already has in ways that will take your breath away. But we have a part to play. God calls us to rise up, shake the dust off, sit enthroned. We have a part to play in our freedom.

Why does anyone choose captivity? Well, captives do get fed. On a regular basis. They're safe in their cages, their cells, their prisons. In the movie *The Shawshank Redemption*, longtime prisoner and now ringleader Red has been incarcerated for decades. He confesses, "These walls are funny. First you hate 'em, then you get used to 'em. Enough time passes, you get so you depend on them."[1]

Prisons can be safe and comfortable. They can become a known life, a familiar way. Resignation is safe; dreaming is dangerous. Letting someone else control your life is easier than rising up to deny them that control; the relationship will never be the same. Living under shame can feel far easier than fighting for your own dignity. The known is always more comfortable and less risky than the unknown. After a while, those animals in the zoo forget they were even made for the open skies, the wild savannas. This is a horrible place to come to. Not a one of us was created to live in captivity.

Let me ask you, dear one: What would you love to be free from? Is it sorrow? Regret? Self-contempt, addiction, shame, fear, worry, doubts?

What would you love to be free to do? Live your life? Follow your dreams? Love with abandon? Worship God? Experience Jesus— follow him, know him, believe him?

As we step more and more into freedom, we become the women we were meant to be. It can happen; it can be yours.

So why would captive Daughter Zion have to be told to free herself from the chains around her neck? We choose captivity over freedom because we are afraid of the price.

When Sabatina James, an eighteen-year-old Pakistani woman, rejected the arranged marriage her parents had made for her, her life became a living hell. After she refused to live within the confines of her family's cultural parameters, her mother began to call her cruel names and beat her while alone or even in larger family gatherings. When the violence escalated and her parents threatened to murder her, she ran away. (The UN estimates that five thousand girls are murdered around the world every year by their parents for acting in ways they feel shame the family.) Living in Germany now, Sabatina said, "I rarely go out alone. I often wonder if someone is lurking around the corner. I have always loved my freedom—but I have paid a high price."[2]

Yes, freedom can be costly. We know that. Look at Jesus. But captivity is always more costly. You pay too high a price to stay in chains. Freedom is good; freedom is what you are made for.

> *It is for freedom that Christ has set us free. Stand firm, then, and do not let yourselves be burdened again by a yoke of slavery.*
>
> Galatians 5:1

We have been given the greatest freedom of all: freedom of heart, freedom from sin, a freedom that enables us to live and love as Jesus did.

We can be free from:

Bondage

Sin

The fear of man

Shame

Regret

Rage

Disappointment

Addiction

Fear

You name it

What would you like to be free from?

We are no longer captives to sin. We are no longer slaves to the Enemy, to the world, or to our own flesh. We have been released. We are not only free *from*; we are free *to*! We are free to be transformed into the very image of Christ. We are free to love in the face of hatred. Free to become the fullest expression of our unique selves. Free to offer to others the beauty that God planted in us when he first dreamed of us. We are free to:

Dream
Be happy
Be glorious
Succeed
Love
Live
Forgive
Not be bound by any chains

We have this freedom because of what Jesus has done for us! We have been ransomed, paid for, saved, and freed to be who we really are and do what we are meant to do.

What would you like to be free to do?

This brings us another startling freedom: we are free to fail. Let me say that again. We are free to fail. Because of Jesus, we can be free from the cages of other people's expectations, demands, yokes, and judgments—even our own.

This isn't about getting it perfect, dear one. We are loved, forgiven, embraced; we live under grace, not under judgment. Grace sets us free from perfectionism, which is a terrible prison. It sets us free even to fail.

My emotions waver. My physical strength and spiritual life have variables. One day I am strong in Christ, believing everything God says, and on another day I am not so strong. That's okay. I will never be free from needing God, and neither will you. He alone is perfect, valiant, complete. And in him, so are we. But only in him.

> Now the Lord is the Spirit, and where the Spirit of
> the Lord is, there is freedom. (2 Cor. 3:17)

freedom from spiritual bondage

The other night I was lying on the floor with worship music playing. But I wasn't lying on the floor worshipping. I was wondering. The day had not been a great one. I was exhausted from work and too many conversations and thought the answer to my physical and emotional state would be found in pizza and chocolate ice cream. I chose to spend the entire day in old patterns of living that have never proven helpful. Lying on the floor, listening to the music, I asked God, "Do you really love me now? Here? How can you possibly love me in this low place?"

But I knew he did. Jesus died on the cross for all of my sins, even the ones I have committed over and over and over again. There was a battle going on for my freedom that day. And it was raging where it almost always rages: over what I would choose to believe.

It wouldn't be right for me to talk about our freedom in Christ without addressing spiritual warfare at least a little bit. In *Waking the Dead*, my husband, John, wrote, "You won't understand your life, you won't see clearly what has happened to you or how to live forward from here, unless you see it as battle. A war against your heart."[3] Jesus has won our freedom in a spiritual showdown with Satan. But our Enemy still refuses to go down without a fight. He knows he cannot take down Jesus, the Victorious One. But he can still wound his heart by wounding ours. Jesus has won our freedom. But we need to receive it, claim it, and stand in it. That is our good fight of faith: believing God is who he says he is and believing we are who he says we are in the face of evidence surrounding us that screams the opposite.

In order for us to live in freedom and become who we are to become, we need to receive God's love even in our lowest places.

Spiritual warfare is designed to separate you from the love of God. Its goal is to keep you from living in the freedom that Jesus has purchased for you. Satan whispers to us when we have failed or sinned or are feeling horrid that we are nothing and no one. He is a liar. And our fight for our freedom involves exposing him for who he is even when the lies feel completely true. The battle is waged and won in our thought life: in our minds and in our hearts.

So what are you thinking? (Yeah, right now.) Descartes famously wrote, "I think, therefore I am." I would add a fill-in-the-blank in each phrase. I think I am ____, therefore I am ____. I think I am kind, therefore I am kind. I think I am chosen, therefore I am chosen. I think I am becoming more loving, therefore I am becoming more loving. I think I am forever bound to sin, therefore I am forever bound to sin. What we think about ourselves, others, or a circumstance informs how we perceive it, which informs the way we experience it. Our thoughts play out in our lives.

> We demolish arguments and every pretension that
> sets itself up against the knowledge of God, and we
> take captive every thought to make it obedient to
> Christ. (2 Cor. 10:5)

What do you think about God? What do you think about yourself? Who are you? What do you think life is about? What do you think is true? Because what you think informs your reality and has a direct effect on how you live your life. What we focus on, we move toward. What we look at and esteem molds us in its direction. What are you thinking?

> Behold, you delight in truth in the inward being.
> (Ps. 51:6 ESV)

> Thy word is truth. (John 17:17 KJV)

> But when he, the Spirit of truth, comes, he will
> guide you into all the truth. (John 16:13)

In order to recognize a lie, we need to know the truth. Experts in counterfeit money don't spend their time studying counterfeits. They study the real currency. In the same way, to engage in the spiritual battle raging around us, we don't shift our focus to lies or to the Devil. We focus on Jesus. We marinate in the truth of who God is and who he says we are. Then and only then will we be able to quickly recognize a lie. And though there are some areas of bondage in our lives where truth is not going to be enough to set us completely free, we will never get any freedom at all without it.

Remember when Jesus was in the wilderness and the Devil came to tempt him? Jesus didn't reason with the Enemy. He didn't engage with him in a dialogue; he simply refuted him with the truth. "Then you will know the truth, and the truth will set you free" (John 8:32).

So, Spiritual Warfare Level One: You have an Enemy. You are hated. Evil exists. Satan exists. Foul spirits exist. Peter wrote, "Be alert and of sober mind. Your enemy the devil prowls around like a roaring lion looking for someone to devour" (1 Pet. 5:8). Devour, not tempt. Devour as in shred, maul, kill, destroy. James commanded, "Submit yourselves, then, to God. Resist the devil, and he will flee from you" (James 4:7).

If we do not submit to God, the Devil will not flee. If we do not resist the Devil, he will not flee. There is no reason to fear or strive. But we do need to submit to God and resist the Devil. We enforce the freedom Jesus has won for us by believing and agreeing with the truth. This is a big, big part of "shake off your dust; rise up, sit enthroned, Jerusalem. Free yourself from the chains on your neck, Daughter Zion, now a captive" (Isa. 52:2). Time to rise up, girl.[4] Spiritual laws need to be enforced just like traffic laws. When you are dealing with fallen angels, think Somali pirates; sex traffickers;

the Mafia; and lawbreakers who hate authority, rebel against it, and breathe death and destruction. Demons don't stop harassing you if you don't force them to stop harassing you.

> *So what are you thinking? Yeah, right now. About this topic. About yourself. Does what you are thinking about yourself, others, or your circumstances today align with the Word of God?*

We can no longer afford to let our thoughts run wild. What we think about matters. We have to make it a practice to regularly check in on our hearts, our thoughts. What are we believing? What agreements are we making? Why? When we become aware that our thoughts are not aligned with the Word of God, we repent and elevate our thoughts to agree with God. When we become aware of agreements we are making with the Enemy, like, "Life is hard, then you die," or "I will never change," we break those agreements regardless of how we feel. Out loud. As in:

I renounce this lie. I break every agreement I have been making with my Enemy. I renounce the agreement that [I am overwhelmed; I'll never get free; I hate so-and-so; I am stupid, ugly, fat, depressed—name it and break with it]. I renounce this in the name of Jesus Christ my Lord.

what is true?

Here are some true things to fill your mind with:

The one who is in you is greater than the one who is in the world. (1 John 4:4)

For he has rescued us from the dominion of darkness and brought us into the kingdom of the Son he loves, in whom we have redemption, the forgiveness of sins. (Col. 1:13–14)

And having disarmed the powers and authorities [spiritual powers and spiritual authorities], he made a public spectacle of them, triumphing over them by the cross. (Col. 2:15)

All authority in heaven and on earth has been given to me. (Matt. 28:18)

But because of his great love for us, God, who is rich in mercy, made us alive with Christ even when we were dead in transgressions—it is by grace you have been saved. And God raised us up with Christ and seated us with him in the heavenly realms in Christ Jesus. (Eph. 2:4–6)

I have given you authority to trample on snakes and scorpions and to overcome all the power of the enemy; nothing will harm you. However, do not rejoice that the spirits submit to you, but rejoice that your names are written in heaven. (Luke 10:19–20)

Daughter of Zion—daughter of the true King—you rise up and sit enthroned when you take your position in Christ and command the Enemy to leave. The Enemy has been disarmed by the cross of Jesus Christ. When we engage in spiritual warfare, *we are enforcing* what has already been accomplished. That's how you free yourself from the chains around your neck!

A basic tool for recognizing if you are under spiritual attack or dealing with foul spirits is to judge the fruit: "By their fruit you will recognize them" (Matt. 7:16). Is misunderstanding coming against your friendships? Pray against that. I bring the cross and blood of Jesus Christ against all misunderstanding and command it bound to his throne—by his authority and in his name. Are you feeling fear? Discouragement? Self-hatred? The fruit of all that is pretty obvious—it is foul, dark, and from hell. Resist it in the name of Jesus.

I am not being simplistic. I understand that often many other issues are involved: our brokenness, our sin, our history. Sometimes there's a reason we struggle with certain things. That's why James says we should first submit to God, then resist the Devil.

For instance, say you keep getting hit hard with a spirit of resentment. Commanding it to leave will not make it go away if you are entertaining resentment in your heart, engaging it in your imagination, and opening the door to it by agreeing with it in your thoughts. First you have to repent of resentment toward others, yourself, and God. Repent. You must seek the healing of Jesus in the wounds that allow resentment to come. You need to choose to love Christ right here, in this very place. This is how you submit to God. Then you will have the authority to command it to leave because you've withdrawn the welcome mat.

Familiar spirits are often hard to recognize because they are historic things you have struggled with. For me, as for many, it would be depression.

We need to break every agreement we have made with Satan. With discouragement. Defeat. Despair. Loneliness. Rage. Self-hatred.

Break agreements with it. Even if it feels true. Especially if it feels true! Repent of entertaining it, making room for it. Then send it to Jesus. I like to send foul spirits to the throne of Christ for him to decide what to do with them. I don't just want to cast them out of my room or my house so they can go on to whomever they desire next. A lot of times, if it's coming against you, it's coming against the others around you as well. Send it to Jesus; forbid its return.

Let's say you walk into a room and are suddenly hit with a wave of fear. Or perhaps you go to bed at night and BOOM, you start worrying about the future, your friends, you name it. Fear. There's a mighty strong chance this isn't just you. The Enemy may well be present in the form of a spirit of fear. When that happens to me, here is how I pray:

I bring the cross and blood of Jesus Christ against all fear, and in the name of Jesus Christ and by his authority I command every spirit of fear to leave me now; I send you bound to the throne of Jesus Christ. Go. Now. In Jesus's name.

It's good to name the specific spirit you are coming under. It doesn't give it more power; rather it's like opening the door into the cellar and letting the light in. It removes the power. You become aware that you aren't overwhelmed or full of fear or shame. You aren't intimidated. You don't want to die. No, that's coming from a foul spirit. Rebuke it. Out loud. In the name of Jesus Christ.

We'd better close this chapter with prayer:

Praise you, Jesus. Thank you for all you have accomplished for us. We love you. We worship you. You are the King of Kings and Lord of Lords, and your name is above every other name that can be given in this age or in the age to come. We come under your authority now. We receive all the work that you accomplished for us in your cross and death, in your resurrection, and in your ascension. We take our place in your authority now, and in your name, Jesus, we come against every foul spirit that has been harassing us. We bring the cross and blood of Jesus Christ against every foul spirit of [what has been attacking you? Hatred, rage, intimidation, shame, accusation, judgment, offense, misunderstanding, fear, panic, dread, hopelessness, despair?]. We bring your blood and cross against these foul spirits. In the name of Jesus Christ and by his authority, we command every foul spirit bound to the throne of Jesus Christ for judgment. We break every agreement we have made with the Enemy, and we renounce them now. We make our agreement with the Truth. Father, please send your angels to enforce this command. Thank you, God. Praise you. We worship you, Jesus. We long to be free, to know you and to love you more deeply and truly. You are worthy. Please remove everything that separates us from knowing you as you truly are and keeps us from living in the freedom that you have purchased for us. In Jesus's mighty name. Amen.

God has done everything, won everything, and given us every-thing we need to live in freedom. We are meant to walk in it, more and more. We won't walk gracefully into it all the time. But by the grace of God, and with his help, we can stumble into it. One thought at a time. One day at a time.

Chapter Eight
a little rain

*It's a good thing to have all the props pulled
out from under us occasionally.
It gives us some sense of what is rock under
our feet, and what is sand.*
Madeleine L'Engle, *Glimpses of Grace*

Henry Wadsworth Longfellow wrote, "Into each life some rain must fall." He failed to mention torrential hail, hurricanes, and floods. What comes into most people's lives is an endless series of severe thunderstorms. Everywhere we look, people are suffering. Even when we look in the mirror. We wake each morning to a new day rife with possibilities, but we have no idea what will come our way. Joy? Sorrow? The "some rain" that Longfellow wrote about threatens to sweep away our capacity to breathe. But God says that he uses all things for our good. Seriously? What good can possibly come from suffering?

finding peace in difficult circumstances

How do you understand your life? Why is it turning out so differently from what you imagined? What do you make of its randomness? The phone rings, and you have no idea what is coming. It could be great news! It could be a friend inviting you to a movie! Maybe you won a car! Or it could be something much different.

In John 16:33 Jesus said, "In this world you will have trouble." Is he not the master of understatement?

Christianity is not a promise to enjoy a life without pain, nor to be given a shortcut through it. It is a promise that pain, sorrow, sin—ours and others'—will not swallow us, destroy us, define us, or have the final word. Jesus has won the victory. And in him so have we.

No one gets a pain-free life. I know some girls' lives look pretty perfect from a distance, but only from a distance. You get close and you learn the truth. A life without suffering is a fantasy life, and you don't live in a fantasy. No, your life is much more the stuff of fairy tales. Really. There are wicked witches in fairy tales. There are dragons. In fairy tales, big bad wolves devour beloved grandmothers, and little girls wander the woods alone and afraid.

Hard times come to everyone. Our current address is far from Eden. We live in a fallen world with broken people, and we ourselves are not yet all that we are meant to be. Life is difficult on most days, but sometimes it is painful beyond measure.

In your life, what have been the most difficult trials for you?

Peter wrote, "Dear friends, do not be surprised at the fiery ordeal that has come on you to test you, as though something strange were happening to you" (1 Pet. 4:12). But we are surprised, aren't we? We wonder, *What did we do wrong?* Or are we wrong about God? What we believe about God is quickly exposed by pain. What's he like, *really?* Is he mean? Is he harsh? Is he mad at us? Does he not care? Does he not see? Did we fall through the cracks of the universe? The very first thing painful trials try to do is separate us from God. But being separated from God is the worst thing that can happen, much worse than the most excruciating of trials.

When suffering comes, we don't want to jump to conclusions. But it is a good idea to ask God, "What is this? What's going on here?"

A terrible flu has swept through our town this season. It hit us hard, but it hit a friend of mine harder. As I talked with her one day, she confessed, "I wish I would learn what God is trying to teach me so I could get over this flu." What was she assuming about God? She was assuming that every sickness is from him. That simply isn't true. We live in a fallen world. The flu goes around. Sickness is not a punishment from God. He is not waiting for her to grasp some deeper truth about herself or to repent of some hidden sin before he heals her. He is not holding out on her (or us) to finally get her act together in order to bless her. He is not a mean God but a loving one filled with grace and mercy. It is his kindness that draws us to repentance, not his cruelty. God will use painful trials, even the flu, to hone us, but he doesn't cause all of them.

Some of my readers will need some help with this because they've been taught a theology that God causes all things. So they have had to swallow hard and accept the view that God caused them to be sexually abused, God caused their mother to die a premature death, God caused their friend to betray them. Oh, friends, this is a horrible view of God and a profound *heresy*. Listen:

> When tempted, no one should say, "God is tempting me." For God cannot be tempted by evil, nor does he tempt anyone; but each person is tempted when they are dragged away by their own evil desire and enticed. Then, after desire has conceived, it gives birth to sin; and sin, when it is full-grown, gives birth to death. (James 1:13–15)

James makes it clear in this passage that God does not tempt anyone to sin, nor does he go on to cause them to sin. But people are tempted every day; they go on to sin every day. So, then, things happen every single day that God is not causing. God does not make anyone sin, but people sin every day, and those sins have terrible consequences. This is not God doing these things. Do you see what an important difference it makes?

In his sovereign power God created a world where the choices of angels and human beings matter. We are not puppets on a string. When someone sins, it is not God causing them to sin. That sexual abuse was not arranged by God. He did not cause your lack of friends any more than he caused those terrorists to bomb the train station.

It is crucial for us to be careful with our interpretation of events. We must ask God's help in making sense of it all. But for heaven's sake, don't blame the sin of the world on God. Ever since Adam and Eve sinned, this world has been badly, badly broken. Not only did sin enter in, but the natural world itself spiraled into brokenness. Disease entered in. Maybe you have a terrible flu because someone sneezed on you or your sister brought it home from school. God did not place those germs for you to get them.

But yes, God can and does use the suffering of this world to shape us. Maybe you have the flu because you have been living your life at breakneck speed and refusing to rest and take care of your body. Maybe. We need to ask Jesus for his interpretation. Your interpretation of the events will shape everything that follows. It will shape your emotions, your perspective, and your decisions. What if you are wrong?

> *Take a moment to ask God to help you make sense of what you are going through right now. Ask him to help you see what is from him in your situation, what is from other people's sin, and what is a result of this fallen world (like the flu). Ask him to help you see what he is doing through the suffering, even if he didn't cause the suffering.*

first things first

I learned long ago that in cases of suffering, you can have understanding or you can have Jesus. If you insist on understanding, you usually lose both.

When suffering enters into your life, take a deep breath. The very first thing to do is to invite Jesus into it. Pray, *Jesus, catch my heart.*

When painful trials come your way, by all means ask God what's up—ask him to interpret them for you. But whether he provides understanding or not, invite Jesus in. Keep inviting Jesus into the pain. Invite Jesus into the places in your heart that are rising to the surface through the suffering, be those painful memories, unbelief, or self-contempt. Pray, *Please come meet me here, Jesus. I need you.*

Let suffering be the door you walk through that draws you to deeper intimacy with Jesus. Suffering can do that, if we let it. And though it would never be the doorway we would choose, it is one we will never regret walking through.

Let me say this again. Let suffering be the door you walk through that draws you to deeper intimacy with Jesus. Let it play its sanctifying role.

Because though God doesn't cause all the trials in our lives, he does use them. He does work all things for our good. He will use pain to expose our false beliefs about our hearts and about his heart. He will use it to prick a place in us that has been wounded here before, to reveal our brokenness so that God can heal it. He will use suffering to reveal Jesus's faithfulness, kindness, and unending love for us.

What is the situation for which you need to pray, "Jesus, catch my heart"?

You see, there is more going on here than meets the eye. There is a battle raging over the human heart. Will we love God and choose to trust the goodness of his heart in the face of the immense brokenness of the world? Will we stand in our belief that God is worthy of our worship and praise in the face of the immense brokenness in our world?

> The Spirit of the Sovereign LORD is on me,
>   because the LORD has anointed me
>   to proclaim good news to the poor.
> He has sent me to bind up the brokenhearted,
>   to proclaim freedom for the captives
>   and release from darkness for the
>   prisoners,
> to proclaim the year of the LORD's favor
>   and the day of vengeance of our God,
> to comfort all who mourn,
>   and provide for those who grieve in
>   Zion—
> to bestow on them a crown of beauty
>   instead of ashes,
> the oil of joy
>   instead of mourning,
> and a garment of praise
>   instead of a spirit of despair.
> They will be called oaks of righteousness,
>   a planting of the LORD
>   for the display of his splendor.
>   (Isa. 61:1–3)

There may not be a more beautiful passage in all of Scripture. If you've read any of my and my husband John's books, you know it is our favorite. Because *this* is what Jesus declared he came to do. He announced that he had come to heal the brokenhearted, to set the captive free. He came to restore us in him and to him. He came to comfort those who grieve, to bestow on them a crown of beauty instead of ashes and a garment of praise instead of a spirit of despair. He says that sorrow may last for the night, but joy comes in the morning. It comes with the morning star. It comes with Jesus. Jesus is the answer. Always.

How do you find peace in the midst of difficult, painful circumstances? Let Peace find you. He's right where you are, right smack-dab in the middle of your life.

In the midst of our joy, our busyness, our sorrow, and our suffering, we must turn our gaze on Jesus. Invite Jesus in. Ask him to prove to us once again that he is who he says he is. He says he is our Strength. Our Shield. Our Rock. Our Hiding Place. Our Refuge. Our Deliverer. Our great Comforter, our faithful Companion, and our ever-present Friend. Jesus says he is the mighty God, the Prince of Peace. We can trust him.

Jesus is the only One who can meet the deepest needs of your heart, and he wants you to know how deeply he loves you so badly that he's moved heaven and earth to do it. He is the only One who will never disappoint you, never, ever leave you, comfort you intimately, and love you perfectly every single moment of your life. Invite him in.

beauty will come

My mother could be a very driven woman; we couldn't walk on the carpet in the living room because we would leave footprints. My mom could be short with me; she could be controlling and demanding; she failed in many ways. Not in every way, not by a long shot, but she did have her rough edges. My mother also loved Jesus. When cancer began to ravage her life, a startling transformation began to take place. My mother softened; she became gentler than she was before—or she became gentle more often. She loosened her grasp on control; it just didn't matter. She lost her edge to demand or criticize. She said "I love you" more than she ever had. The beauty that was always there began to come forth in truly amazing ways. Our last four months together were the best months of love and relationship we ever shared.

My mother suffered intensely during the last months of her life. She had suffered much in the long years prior to them as well. But in those final months, she leaned into God and came to know his love in a way that filled her heart with peace, rest, and joy. Unable to swallow anything, my mom received nourishment via a feeding tube. A tiny sip of water was impossible for her to take down. She hoped that when she crossed over from life to Life, Jesus would be waiting for her with a large, cold glass of water.

My mom kept a diary all her life. Not journals, diaries; little entries of how she spent her days. A few months after she died, I was reading through her diary from her last year of life when a note in her precious handwriting fell out. This is what it said:

I wish to thank the beautiful priests and parishioners at St. Edwards Church and San Felipe de Jesus for their prayers during my illness. I had an unexpected diagnosis, and it has been the most awesome, rewarding, and glorious time God has ever given to me. I thank God the Father, Son, and Holy Spirit from the depth of my soul.

Mary Jane Morris

My mother actually gave thanks in her suffering—not for the suffering, but for what it did in her life. It opened her up to relationship; it caused her to see the value of love over clean carpets and a neat kitchen; it enabled her to offer love and receive love. And though her battle with cancer ended up costing her life, what she gained through the pain she named "the most awesome, rewarding, and glorious time God has ever given to me."

And she's drinking Living Water now!

I am surrounded by people who are surrendering their lives to Jesus in deeper ways. They may not understand why things have happened as they have, but they are trusting God that no matter what, he is good. Our friend Scott has grown to know and trust God profoundly. He sent us a little note on the twenty-eighth anniversary of his fall from a ladder that left him paralyzed from the waist down. He simply wrote, "No regrets." The note brought John and me to tears.

God didn't give my mom cancer any more than he caused Scott to fall. He didn't cause it. But he will use it. He will use it to reveal to us who he really is in the face of tragedy and anguish. He will use it to reveal to us who we really are. Jesus wants us to know who we are. He wants us to see ourselves as our Father sees us. The most important mirror for us to look in is our reflection in his eyes.

I would like to become a woman who is as desperate for God in my joy as I am in my sorrow. That has not happened yet. Nothing brings my heart to fully run after God like being in a season of grief. It may be grief over the way I have failed my sons or my husband. It may be sorrow over a revelation of how my selfishness has hurt my friends. It may be pain over the suffering that one I love is experiencing. But nothing causes me to seek God like pain.

thank you

I don't pretend that suffering always has a good effect on us. I've known women made hard, angry, and jealous by their suffering. They envied those who did not seem to be suffering as they were; they even went so far as to wish suffering upon them so that "they would know what it's like." This is tragedy; this is ugly. We never, ever want to wish suffering upon another person.

How do we allow suffering to do a holy work in us and not let it make us envious, hard, or angry?

First, I think we need to be honest about what we have done with our suffering. What have we allowed it to do to our hearts? Have we become more fearful? Controlling? Has resentment toward God or others entered in? Let us quickly bring that to Jesus, for this is cancer of the soul, and it ravages what God means to make lovely. We renounce our anger or envy, our controlling or bitterness. We bring it quickly under the blood of Jesus and ask him to remove it all from our heart and soul.

We also need his healing love. We ask him to do in us the very thing he promised in Isaiah 61:

Jesus, heal my broken heart, release me from all darkness. Comfort me in my suffering. Cleanse me from all evil that has gotten in or taken root in the places of my sorrow. Comfort me. Give me a crown of beauty instead of ashes; make me beautiful here, Lord, in this. Give me the oil of gladness instead of mourning; lift my grief and sorrow and give me the oil of your gladness; give me a garment of praise instead of a spirit of despair. Rescue me.

I think we can hasten this process of healing. I think it begins with that last phrase about praise instead of despair. Nothing—nothing—undoes the harmful effects of suffering as our choice to begin to love and worship Jesus in the midst of it.

Worship him in it. Be thankful to him in it.

Which is not the same thing as being thankful for it.

The Scriptures don't tell us to give thanks to God for every wicked, evil, hard, painful, excruciating, grief-filled thing that happens in our or others' lives. That is not what it means. That would be calling evil good. And we are also told by Scripture never, ever to do that. No, what the Scripture says is this: "Rejoice always, pray continually, give thanks in all circumstances; for this is God's will for you in Christ Jesus" (1 Thess. 5:16–18).

Give thanks to God in every situation, not for every situation.

By loving Jesus in our pain, we allow him into our pain.

Being thankful opens up windows in the spiritual realm for the presence of God to fill our lives, our thoughts, our understanding, and our perspective. It opens up the doors to the blessings that God wants to pour into our lives. We will come to a place of increasing gratefulness for the story of our lives, both the joyful times and the excruciating seasons. The golden moments that we cherish forever and the awful moments we can't seem to forget. We are on our way to the place of being able to exalt God over all of it. Yes, all of it.

In *Jesus Calling*, Sarah Young wrote,

> Thankfulness is not some sort of magic formula; it
> is the language of Love, which enables you to com-
> municate intimately with Me. A thankful mind-set

does not entail a denial of reality with its plethora
of problems. Instead, it rejoices in Me, your Savior,
in the midst of trials and tribulations. I am your refuge and strength, an ever present and well proved
help in trouble.[1]

When Jesus rose from the dead and appeared to his disciples,
Thomas was not present. So Jesus came back to them again, when
Thomas was also in their midst. Do you recall how Jesus proved that he
was real, and risen, and still the same Jesus they had always known and
loved? He told Thomas, "Put your hands in my scars." Jesus still had
his scars then, and he still has them today. They are Jesus's glory. They
are what we most worship him for. Glorified Jesus still has his scars,
and when we reach glory, so will we. But they will be beautiful, like his.

The story of my life and the struggles I have lived with—make
that live with—have helped to shape me into the woman I am today
and the woman I am becoming. My scars, my struggles, my failures,
my joys, my private, lonely agonies have been forging my soul into
something beautiful. Eternal. Good. Yours have too.

Now, we can fight that process—or we can yield to it. My dear
mother had her rough edges; you have yours; I have mine. We can
choose to let suffering soften us or harden us. We can choose whether
we will allow it to make us more compassionate or let our hearts
become jealous of others. We can choose whether we will love Jesus
in it or resent him for it. Only one set of choices will make us more
beautiful.

The pain we experience, the sorrow and the agony, serve a purpose. God is working all things together for our good. He is etching

a masterpiece of stunning design. The beauty being forged in us through the transforming work of suffering is one that will leave us breathless, stunned, and forever thankful. And the crowning glory will be that because of the pain we have endured, we have come to know Jesus in a way that causes us to treasure the trial as one of God's greatest gifts to us. Amazing.

> *What would you love to be the fruit of the suffering you are currently enduring or have endured in the past? Pray and ask God for that fruit.*

Chapter Nine

friendship

*A true friend never gets in your way unless
you happen to be going down.*

Arnold H. Glasow

My friend ate a slug once.

She and her friends came upon it while they were exploring the
fields by her home. They rolled over a stump and there it was in all
of its bulbous, slimy glory. "I dare you to eat it."

We need friends. Of course we do. We are image bearers of the living God, and one of the best ways our feminine hearts bear his image
is in our desire for relationship. We are relational to our core. Just like
God, we have a deep desire and capacity for relationship, and just like
God, we want to be chosen and wanted. We want to be pursued by
others not for what we can do but for who we are. It's a good desire.
And one that can get us into trouble if we aren't aware of it.

People get into all kinds of trouble with peer pressure. Caving
in to doing things, saying things, wearing things, even eating

things that they don't really want to because they want to belong. Be included. Fit in. Be a part of the group! "Do it! I dare you."

I was driving last summer with some gals, all of whom are really pretty and slender and smart and have a lot of friends. (So, yeah, intimidating gals.) I risked asking them the question, "Do you feel like you fit in?" Looking at their lives from the outside, I expected their answers to be, "Yes. Sure!" None of them said that. All five, after a lengthy pause and with lowered voices, confessed, "No. I don't."

Okay, then. The cat's out of the bag.

We share the feeling of being odd. Weird. In our inner worlds, we feel alone. And being alone is the first thing that God named as "not good" (Gen. 2:18).

We share an ache in our hearts that no one can fill and a fear that if people really knew us, they would run away as fast as they could! We share that. We share the feeling that most everyone else has it together and we are barely pulling it off. We share the feeling that we don't fit in.

One of the reasons to read this book and even talk about it with others is to pull back the curtain on your inner world and let you know that you are not weird! You are not alone! Really. Honestly. And you are not meant to live alone. You need a couple of friends to share this life with. Friends who may look like they have it all together and fit in or don't care if they do or not (but who do care, really), and who feel much the same as you.

Friends are necessary. They can be hard to come by. They can wound and hurt and betray. Certainly they will disappoint sometimes. That comes with the territory of being human.

Friends can also bless and enrich and deepen every experience of life with joy.

> *The next best thing to being wise oneself is to*
> *live in a circle of those who are.*
> C. S. Lewis, *Selected Literary Essays*

A good friend loves you when you are hilarious and when you are hurting. A true friend loves you when you are being kind and when you are PMS-ing all over the place. She may not love what you are doing, or the dragon you are manifesting, but she loves you. She knows who the true you is, and even in the midst of your living as an imposter to your very self, a friend calls you up and out. A friend sees who you are meant to be and beckons you to rise to the higher version of yourself.

Friendship is a high and holy thing, and a two-way street. Friendships are also messy. They are not for the faint of heart.

I have learned a few things about friendships over the years, and where I have made mistakes, I have made colossal ones. I'd love to spare you that, as much as possible anyway. What I have learned, I offer to you.

be careful with your expectations

Sometimes I am absolutely amazed at how much Jesus loves people. Some days—okay, most days—people can be pretty odd. We are all living on the island of misfit toys, and most of us are not even aware that one of our wheels is in the shape of a square.

We bump into each other. We step on each other's toes, and then what is one to do?

Friendships can be hard. They are opposed by the Enemy. They need to be fought for. Anything worth having and cherishing is.

For many years, I thought that a cherished best, best friend would understand me at all times and enjoy all the same things I enjoy. She'd want to go to a movie when I wanted to go to a movie, and she would want to see the same show I wanted to see. She would think I was amazing and wise and justified in my mood swings. She would be available to me whenever I called and only be encouraging and empathetic. She would be passionate about the same causes I am passionate about. She would always get my jokes and want to eat at the same restaurant I wanted to eat at, and she would never be offended by a failure of mine. Oy! And, yeah, I know, embarrassing, right?

But Oprah has Gayle. Rachel has Monica. Anne with an "e" has Diana. Aren't they all that for each other? I'm whining now.

Actually, I am being ridiculous. Because I have amazing friends, friends who are the best. And I am learning that each of these variously gifted friends offers something of unique value that the others don't. Their very differences from each other and from me enrich my life! No one woman could possibly be everything to me. God is meeting my need for friendship, just not through one person. Some girls are blessed with a best friend. But most aren't. Most of us have a few friends who provide something we need, and we provide something they need. Our hearts are met in many ways by the beautiful offerings of a few. I don't think a human being is actually able to bear the burden of being someone's one and only. God alone can be our One and Only.

God understands us all the time. He is available every moment. People don't and aren't. They have lives and schedules and a myriad of people pulling on them, and that makes them normal and not at our beck and call. Jesus calls us "friend." Oh, to know him more deeply as that. I want to know him as my King and my God and my Friend who enjoys me fully, accepts me completely, and loves me unconditionally. Because that is who he is.

Is the thought that Jesus would love to be your closest friend a new one to you? Spend some time and ask him to become that.

hold your friends loosely, but hold them

Just like every other thing of value, friendship is risky and costly. Friendship is meant to provide a refuge from loneliness and a respite from self-criticism and the critique of a never-satisfied world. Friendship is a relationship of mutual enjoyment. It is a place where our hearts don't have to work quite so hard to be heard and understood and accepted. Friendship is supposed to offer a place of rest.

Friendship is a gift, one that each of us is meant to enjoy and offer. We need each other. But in order to continue to move toward one another and receive freely what others are meant to share with us, we need Jesus. Coming to know Jesus more truly as my primary forever Friend is freeing my heart to offer and receive the amazing gift of friendship. He is the only one who will never disappoint, betray, be unavailable, or judge us. He is with us and for us. Always.

Jesus has promised to never leave you or forsake you. He is the same yesterday, today, and forever. He is perfect love, and he loves you perfectly. And he's not going anywhere.

People do go. Friendships change. People change. You change. You are supposed to. You may still be walking in the same direction in life as a dear friend, but your paths may no longer cross. The natural and easy ways that we as friends connect shift under our feet, and it takes enormous effort on both sides for the friendship to shift and continue as well. Perhaps the friendship is meant to continue. Perhaps it isn't. Some friends we are called to fight for, and some we are called to release.

I was at a Graham Cooke conference a number of years ago when he taught about how our friendships change and how normal that is. He said most friendships last three to five years. Really? And, he said, they are meant to have a duration of three to five years. Not every friend in our lives is meant to walk with us through the remainder of our lives. Oh, we love them still. And though all change feels like loss, it is good to bless people on their way, to hold them loosely, and to let them go.

The ironic thing is, I was at that conference with a close friend who I deeply loved and who I was not holding with a loose hand but with a clenched fist. We had been friends for many years, and I assumed we would be friends for the rest of our lives. I ignored the telltale signs of change. This friend had been moving away from me for quite a long while, but I absolutely refused to see it.

I wanted what I wanted. I thought she was fabulous. Surely she must feel the same way about me!

Somewhere along the way, my desire for relationship turned into demand, and demand is one of the death knells of a friendship—of any relationship, really. I needed to unclench my fist and in love let my friend go. I also needed to invite Jesus into the places of my heart that had refused to see that it was time to let her go.

Insisting. Demanding. Refusing. I promise you, those are not verbs that lead to the life Jesus has for us.

Not every girl or guy in your life is going to stay in your life for the duration of it. Not every person you long to have a friendship with is even meant to be your friend. (Sorry. Now take a big, deep breath.) It can be excruciating to let a friend go, or worse, to be let go of. Many people underestimate the closeness of heart that girlfriends are capable of reaching. How well I remember sobbing in the arms of a precious friend when my family was moving across the country. It felt like my heart was being torn out. And we loved each other. How much worse it is when a friendship ends because of offenses, misunderstandings, anger, or betrayal. How searingly painful it is when God calls you to walk away from a cherished friend when love and unity have left the relationship.

We are meant to grow and change and become throughout the duration of our lives, and we need to be surrounded by people who celebrate the person we are becoming. Our true friends are people who are our biggest cheerleaders and encourage us on to the next higher version of ourselves whom God is calling us up to. Friends delight in one another's successes and blessings and are vigilant against jealousy and envy.

Jealousy and envy are two additional death knells to a friendship. God does not want us to be jealous of what our friends receive or achieve. We are called to rejoice with them. We want the best for our friends always and only. Walking with a friend through trials requires much tenderness, grace, and wisdom on our part, but it is actually more difficult to walk with a friend through a season of success and blessing. "She was voted Most Popular. No one even notices me." "I wish I had been given the scholarship." "I love her new clothes. I wish I had new clothes." Careful.

Truth be told, a good part of our transformation takes place in the sanctifying work of relationships. And not because friendship is always a greenhouse, either. Trees grow strong because of winds; drought forces their roots to go deeper. There isn't anything on earth like relationships to make you holy. When our frail humanity is revealed in some way we and others don't like, we bring it to God. We ask for forgiveness. We ask for his life to fill us and his love to flow through us. Which means "Christ in me, love through me" becomes a regular prayer.

It always comes back to Jesus. Jesus. Jesus. Jesus.

When have you been hurt by girlfriends? What happened? How has that shaped your current relationships?

forgive offenses

Misunderstanding one another is so easily and frequently done, it's a miracle any relationship survives. The only way is love. Paul says love "keeps no record of wrongs" (1 Cor. 13:5). In loving relationships, we want to throw away the list in our heads of wrongs done to us and ignore them when they raise their indictments yet again. Too often we keep those lists, ruminate on them, and nurse them like a wounded animal. We say we forgive—and we may even believe we have—but when the list presents itself again, we entertain it with a sort of sick satisfaction. "See what she did? Remember what she said?" We have taken the bait of offense. We are inside the trap.

The word used in Scripture for offense actually means "bait," the bait that is placed inside a trap to lure an animal to its death.

Offenses need to be forgiven quickly, or they will fester and poison the relationship. The poison seeps out and affects our own souls as well. Offenses that are held on to lead to death.

People will hurt us. We will hurt and offend as well. We all will do this with intention and without, with our thoughts bent to wound and with no thought at all. Jesus took all our offenses into his broken body when he died for us, and he took everyone else's as well. All that he suffered—the beating, the scourging, the mocking, and finally the crucifixion—was more than enough to pay for it all. Our offenses and theirs.

With the help of God, we must choose to forgive. Let it go. Let them go. Come out of the trap.

Dear God, I forgive all those who have hurt me, and I bless them in Jesus's name. I pray only more of you to them, for them. And, God, I forgive myself for having hurt others. Please fill me with your Spirit and live and love through me that I might become a woman after your heart who loves others well. In Jesus's name. Amen.

mean girls

There's a reason they made a movie with the title *Mean Girls*. It's because girls can be vicious. They can bully. Ann Shoket, editor-in-chief of *Seventeen* magazine, said girls are adept at ripping apart the social fabric of other girls' lives. Girls can "ice" each other out in their insecure need to feel they are above another girl. Girls bully other girls by getting someone "out" socially and getting others on "their side." They use Facebook groups or Formspring to bully someone anonymously. The effect is both powerful and cruel.[1]

You know the saying "Sticks and stones may break my bones but words will never hurt me" is a flagrant lie. Words wound. Proverbs 18:21 says, "The tongue has the power of life and death," and don't we know it? We are female. We use words. So does God. He is the Word. We are meant to follow his lead and use our words to bless and encourage and bring life.

We can do that! How exciting to think that we can partner with the Holy Spirit in creating little islands of hope and kindness and faithful friends amid the sea of unkindness that too many girls experience.

be careful with the truth

> *It is important to our friends to believe that we are unreservedly*
> *frank with them, and important to friendship that we are not.*
> Mignon McLaughlin, *The Complete Neurotic's Notebook*

A word about honesty. Scripture exhorts us to speak the truth in love. Speak the truth in love. Which means, don't speak the truth in anger or resentment or with the desire to wound. We need to be careful to check our motives underneath our speaking the truth. We want to be aware of the "why" behind the desire to share something. We want to know that we are speaking the truth with the desire to love, to bless. A dear friend told me that when we don't speak the truth in love, *it is no longer truth.*

And Scripture does not exhort us to speak everything that is true. In our culture of honesty, we may feel compelled to share everything with our close friends, even the negative things. We want to be honest, right? We don't want to have secrets from each other, right? Wrong. To share with one you love or are friends with every thought or emotion that goes through your head wreaks havoc on the relationship.

I have really blown it here. I told a good friend about negative feelings I had held about her. I had been jealous of her and the friendship she had with someone that I had wanted to have a friendship with too. I felt edged out. Three's a crowd and all that. When I realized the unreality of those emotions in the face of the truth—that I loved this friend—I confessed them to her. I told her how untrue those feelings were. I was sorry for them.

Right. That went over well. Yes, confession is good for the soul, but confession to whom? And good for whose soul? Not to the person you had hurtful thoughts about! Please be shaking your head, saying, "I can't believe Stasi was that stupid to do that." I can't believe it either. But I was. I have asked for forgiveness. But you know as well as I do that words once spoken cannot be unspoken. Wounds can be healed. Damage can be addressed. Forgiveness can be bestowed. Words cannot be erased.

As we grow into the fullness of who we are created to be, we want to speak only the truth that God calls us to speak, in love, and only when he calls us to speak it.

> *Are there any thoughts or feelings that you need to tell yourself the truth about, but that would be unloving to say to your friend?*

discern and break unholy ties

Okay, if you're skipping ahead or skimming this chapter, stop here. This is really important stuff that is rarely talked about. With some people it feels as if they are sucking the life out of you. That is because they *are* sucking the life out of you. There is an ungodly tie there. You need to break it.

There is some debate and misunderstanding about whether or not Scripture teaches about "soul ties." Let's try to clear that up. However you want to describe it, the Bible clearly teaches that there are holy and unholy bonds between people. Adam and Eve had a holy bond; they became one. (Clearly this goes way beyond "flesh," as any married couple can tell you, especially those married for many years. The bond is at a soul level as well as physical.) Jonathan and David had a very special bond: "After David had finished talking with Saul, Jonathan became one in spirit with David, and he loved him as himself " (1 Sam. 18:1). The King James Version translates it this way: "The soul of Jonathan was knit with the soul of David." So bonds between people can clearly be formed.

When Paul warned about being "yoked" with unbelievers, he was describing an unholy bond. When he warned believers not to have sexual relations outside of marriage, he warned against uniting with that person—clearly a type of bond, an unholy bond. But unholy bonds take place outside of sexual relations too. You've seen relationships where one girl (or guy) holds too much sway over another.

When a friend controls another through moods or threats (unspoken or spoken), there is an ungodly soul tie present. Given our vulnerability as girls and women, given our deep capacity for relationship, we must be aware of the power of unholy ties.

When someone is worrying about you, angry with you, or judging you, and when those emotions cause that person to obsess over you and hold conversations with you when you aren't even present, that creates an unholy bond. This is clearly not the bond of love by the Holy Spirit that Paul said is good; this is an unhealthy bond. These types of unhealthy ties create all sorts of havoc. They form a kind of spiritual walkway over which another person's spiritual warfare travels to you. The negative emotions, demonic strongholds, or accusing spirits that have been accosting that person come over and accost you. The soul tie is a two-way street, by the way, so what you are struggling with goes over to her as well.

Galatians 6:14 declares that through the cross of Christ, "the world has been crucified to me, and I to the world." The cross changes every relationship. Even family ties. "Anyone who loves their father or mother more than me is not worthy of me; anyone who loves their son or daughter more than me is not worthy of me. Whoever does not take up their cross and follow me is not worthy of me" (Matt. 10:37–38). All ties are subject now to the rule of Christ. And so we can say, in a very godly and healthy way, "I am crucified to the world, and the world is crucified to me. I am crucified to my mom, to my sister, to my friend, and to my enemy, and they are crucified to me."

The only bond we are urged to maintain is the bond of love by the Holy Spirit. All others—well, it's time to break them. You won't believe how free you can be and how good you can feel!

It is very important to note that breaking a soul tie with people is not the same thing as *rejecting* those people. It is actually the *loving* thing to do. You don't want them obsessing about you, and you don't want to be obsessing about them. You don't want them controlling you, and you don't want to be controlling them. You do not want any further conversations with them when they aren't even there, and you don't want them doing this with you. You certainly don't want their spiritual warfare, and they don't want yours.[2]

This simple prayer will help:

By the cross of Jesus Christ I now sever all soul ties with [name her] in the name of Jesus Christ. I am crucified to her, and she is crucified to me. I bring the cross of Christ between us, and I bring the love of Christ between us. I send [name her]'s spirit back to her body, and I forbid her spiritual warfare to transfer to me or to my domain. I command my spirit back into the Spirit of Jesus Christ in my body. I release [name her] to you, Jesus. I entrust her to you. Bless her, God! In Jesus's name. Amen.

friend me

Social media is here to stay. It has its good points and its dangers. It's a useful way to stay connected and to share life. But it is not a substitute for face-to-face, eye-to-eye connection. You can have hundreds of friends online. You can't maintain that many in the real world. And you need to be grounded in the real world.

There are circles of friendship. Jesus had them. You need them. Maybe there are one to three girls that you are really close to. Girls you trust with the details of your life. Your inner world and your outer one. Then there is a larger circle of, say, ten to fifteen who you are somewhat current with and love to hang out with, but whom you would not call at three in the morning. They're in your youth group, your neighborhood, or your school. Then there is the larger circle of acquaintances. Folks you pass in the hall and say hi to. Friends in your Spanish class or on your soccer team. That is all well and good and normal. You need all of them.

Friends are gifts to us straight from the heart of God to our own, and no one is better at giving perfect gifts than he is. That's what friends are. They are gems to be treasured. Friends lend each other their clothes, their lecture notes, their courage, their ideas, their faith, and their hope. Ralph Waldo Emerson said, "The only way to have a friend is to be one." So let's be one. Let's pray for them. Let's offer kindness and compassion to them. Let's speak the truth in love. Let's forgive them when they hurt or fail us. Let's offer and invite and be the friend to others that we want them to be to us. And all the while, let's entrust our heart to our Forever Friend, Jesus, who truly loves us at all times.

Do you have the kind of friends you wish you had? If not, pray and ask God for them. How can you become a better friend?

those boys!

He really was beautiful. I know boys aren't supposed to be, but he was.
John Green, *The Fault in Our Stars*

I belong to that rare breed of girls who met her husband in high school. In my junior year, I took roll for the teacher in my drama class. One day, this guy named John came up to me, took my hand, and said, "Stasi. *Love.*" I said, "What do you want?" He said, "I'm leaving class today. Please don't mark me absent."

And so our friendship was born. He asked me not to mark him absent a *lot*. Some days I complied. Some days I didn't. He never knew which was which and never asked. John was a rascal. He was a modern-day pirate who threw the Frisbee on the lawn at lunch like a Greek god and whose presence commanded the stage as well as any legendary Shakespearean actor. He was magnetic and I was drawn to him. He was trouble and I was in it.

The next year we shared drama class again, and my heart would skip a beat when John walked into the room. His presence made me feel charged with electricity. Any words he spoke to me felt thick with meaning, and I would ruminate over them for hours. A look, a smile, or a nod from him and I melted inside. I let him know that if he ever needed a ride home, he could ask me.

He started asking.

I love the story of our romance. Now I should say that we began to date, went to prom, went to college, got engaged, and then got married. Wouldn't that be nice? That is not our story. I was mad about John my senior year. He did not share my feelings. A year later, he pursued me, but I didn't trust him. For several years our relationship was hit but mostly miss, yet somehow I managed to survive the storms of unrequited love, hurt feelings, and long distance. It wasn't until I was twenty-one years old that—well, that's a long story for another time, but can I just say … *BOYS!*

They sure make life interesting. Like a roller-coaster ride is interesting.

different is good

The first thing the Bible tells us about people is that we are made in the image of God. "In the image of God he created them" (Gen. 1:27). The second thing we learn is that we are either male or female. "Male and female he created them" (v. 27). Gender is at the core of humanity. As a young woman, you are feminine. Guys are masculine. In the deepest part of their souls, not merely in their bodies, guys are *guys*. And guys—though of equal value and dignity to girls—are something quite "other" from them. But you knew that already.

Guys are different from girls inside and out. From the very beginning. Brain development, brain chemistry, and hormone levels vary by gender while infants are developing in the womb. Guys have hearts like yours with the same deepest longing—to be loved—but their other core questions, their core desires, and their fears take a different form.

Remember, every child enters the world with a question that needs an answer. It is simply this: "Am I loved?" Little girls ask the question (primarily of their father), "Do you delight in me? Am I special? Am I captivating?" Boys ask something else. They don't need to know they are delighted in. They need to know they are strong. Their question is more along the lines of, "Do I have what it takes? Am I the real deal?"

Our core questions are different, and so are our core fears. A girl's deepest fear is abandonment. (Isn't it true? At some deep level, don't you fear being abandoned and alone? That's because you are made to never be alone. You are relational to your very center.) A guy's deepest fear is failure. Being futile. Not being strong enough. Not having what it takes to make an impact for good. Not being able to handle tough situations—a flat tire, a bully, or a crying girlfriend.

Infant boys are more drawn to pictures of crowds than photos of an individual, while baby girls are more drawn to gaze at an individual face. Infant girls prefer to gaze at faces, while infant boys prefer looking at something that *moves* (like a mobile over the crib). Though their motor skills as children reach milestones at the same time, infant boys move more (wiggling and stretching) than infant girls. Boys' physical strength buds earlier. More ER visits happen with boys than with girls. Baby girls are more verbal. They coo more. They talk more. So do women. Some studies say that women speak on average thirteen thousand more words in a day than men do.

It is not all a sociological by-product of how we raise sons and daughters differently from each other (though we do). Biology plays a large part. Gender is at the core of every human being. Scientists and sociologists alike are still trying to figure out how much of the differences stem from biology and how much from socialization, but by far most little boys prefer to move something and little girls prefer to nurture it.

We are different. Different is good.

Generally speaking, girls mature emotionally at a younger age than guys do. (You knew this already, didn't you? Guys are from some other planet. "Girls are from Mars because they're stars. Boys are from Jupiter because they're"… different.) Girls think about relationships more. If you ask a guy what he is thinking and he says, "Nothing," he actually means it. Really.

the talk

The other day I noticed two pairs of people about fourteen years old crossing the street. From a block away I could tell that the girls were trying to allure the attention of the guys. And the guys? They were clueless. They were bantering with each other and trailing a bit behind. They didn't know how to act with or talk to those girls. All four of them were visibly uncomfortable walking in this new terrain of budding interest.

Okay, so let's talk about sex a minute.

Guys generally mature sexually at a younger age than girls do. Their hormones kick in earlier than yours. Guys are more visually stimulated by the opposite sex, and girls are more emotionally stimulated. Studies show that guys peak in sexual desire around age eighteen and women peak in their forties. You can see there's the potential for some conflict here. That simple difference has gotten many a young woman into trouble. The saying "Girls give sex to get love; guys give love to get sex" proved true in my life, and it didn't go well for me.

My experiences with the opposite sex in middle school and high school weren't so great. When I was fifteen, I was thrilled when a young man noticed me and asked me out on a date. I didn't know then how much I was looking to the guy to validate me as a young woman. If he wanted me, then I must be worth wanting. If he thought I was pretty, then maybe I was. I handed over the report card of my life to the guy, and that was a bad move. Actually, it's a bad move to hand over the report card on who you are to anyone, girl or guy, friend or parent. The only person who has the right to tell you who you are and how valuable you are is God. And he has spoken.

But I didn't know that in high school. All I knew was that this first young man in my life was the cute star of the basketball team and he wanted me, so TA DA! I also didn't know that this first boyfriend of mine wasn't that at all. He was actually on a dare to see how far he could go with me and planned to share all the intimate details with the rest of the team. To say that hurt or was embarrassing to me is a very large understatement. I didn't want sex. I wanted love. I didn't get it.

Helpful hint: If a young man says to you, "Don't worry, I won't bite," back away. Because, yes, he will.

Another mistake I made in high school, and many of my friends made it too, was to shift too much power to the guys while robbing it from the girls. What did this or that guy think, say, do, ask? Those were the engrossing questions. Girlfriends were sacrificed on the altar of "I've got a boyfriend now." Friendships that may have lasted for years were set aside in the interest of a relationship with a guy that may have lasted barely a few months or even days. Something inside of too many of us handed away our self-worth to the cutest guy who made our heart skip a beat. Yikes. Treasure your girlfriends. Those friendships have the potential to last a lot longer and ultimately matter a lot more than the romances do.

Now let's really get into it. How far do you think it's okay to go? Base-wise, I mean. What about if you really love each other? What do your friends think? What would your parents say? What does God say?

It's pretty popular in Christian circles these days to hold to the letter of the law. The Bible is cut-and-dried about sexual intercourse outside of marriage. It's called fornication and is a big, unambiguous no. Where some people are getting into trouble is in thinking that though sexual intercourse is not what God wants, everything and anything else is a go. You may have heard that vaginal penetration is against the will of God but oral sex is fine. Every other base is sanctioned but the fourth one. Wrong.

That is what is called following the letter of the law but not the spirit of the law. Sexual intimacy of all kinds is neither wise nor sanctioned outside of the marriage bed. Sexual purity, sexual integrity is one of your greatest gifts. It's to be guarded and treasured. Remember Proverbs 4:23: "Guard your heart, for everything you do flows from it." Remember ungodly soul ties? We are emotional creatures, and where our bodies go, so do our hearts.

This topic is so vital that I cannot begin to do it justice in a mere section of one chapter, so I suggest that you talk honestly about this with adults you trust. As I said earlier, one book that is really good and thorough for you to read is *Every Young Woman's Battle* by Shannon Ethridge and Stephen Arterburn. It goes into detail about your sexuality.

Your sexuality is awakening in this season, and if not, it will be soon. It's a gift from God to be honored. Not used. Not abused. And not wielded. Honored.

know your power

One day in the tenth grade, coming home on the bus, I was getting a lot of attention from the boys around me. I was wearing a T-shirt I hadn't worn before, and I didn't think a thing of it. They did.

A guy friend I had known for five years called me that night and asked if he could come over. I thought that was weird but said, "Sure." He asked to go into the backyard to talk, but once we were alone, he was all over me. It was as though he'd been taken over by an alien! Who was this guy? What was happening?

What was happening was that my T-shirt had revealed a previously unseen breast size. I had the same thing happen in college when I wore a certain pair of really tight jeans. The response I got from the guys around me was crazy. Those jeans were dangerous. They were—or I was—powerful in them. I needed to know it. And so do you.

Your beauty, your body, and your sexuality are powerful. They have a powerful effect on the opposite sex. More than you now realize. It's wonderful but not to be used as a weapon. That backfires on a girl.

You've seen it done, haven't you? A girl who is desperate for love, though she may not even know it, experiences attention from guys, and it feels wonderful so she dresses and acts in ways that allure them. She sacrifices her integrity to them. She feels she is valued because they want her. She's in trouble. She's using sex to get love. She's wielding her sexuality as her superpower to get what she wants. But she isn't actually getting what she really wants. Sex does not equal love.

Love is good. Love is grand. Sexual attraction is a gift. Actually it's holy ground. You are holy ground. So is he. So treat him the way you want to be treated and require that you be treated with respect as well.

When a guy smiles at you, it can make your day. When a guy pursues you (if he is the one you like), it can make you so happy. The problem is that rejection from a guy can break your heart. You don't want to give to young men the power to tell you who you are—how valuable, how lovely, or how wanted. They don't have the right to validate you as a woman.

They cannot answer the deepest questions of your heart. Only God your Father can do that. Your soul is meant to live in a place of security. You are to know you are forever surrounded by love every moment of your life. You are good. You are wanted. You are beautiful. You are chosen. You are pursued. Jesus has done everything, given everything, and won everything to win you. Because you are everything to him.

Guys are fabulous, and romantic relationships are thrilling. But even in the best of times, your heart needs to know you are loved and wanted outside and apart from everyone and anything else. Relationships change. God doesn't. His love is the only forever and always safe place for your heart.

i love guys!

> *"Also, I'm a guy. And guys do different stuff."*
> *"Like ride bikes?" I said.*
> *"No," he replied. "Like have food fights. And break stuff.*
> *And set off firecrackers on people's front porches. And ..."*
> *"Girls can't set off firecrackers on people's front porches?"*
> *"They can," he said ... "but they're smart*
> *enough not to. That's the difference."*
> Sarah Dessen, *Along for the Ride*

You may be starting to feel that I think guys are dangerous. I don't. I think they're wonderful. Giving your heart away is dangerous. Giving your body away is dangerous. But guys? They're awesome. I love them. (I'm the mother to three fabulous ones.) There are really good ones out there who are strong, kind, noble, deep, handsome, caring, funny, adventurous, creative, brave, and have amazing and good hearts. Even so, they're a grand mystery.

(What I think is hilarious is that they think we are the mystery. Hah! Well, to be fair, we are sometimes even a mystery to ourselves. Mystery isn't bad. Hooray for mystery, or, as the French say, *"Vive la différence!"*)

Boys think it's fun to wrestle. They greet each other with a punch. They like to climb higher, jump farther, and ratchet up the danger level to make things more fun. The riskier, the better. They need friends, just as girls do, but they don't sit and talk and play with each other's hair. They do stuff. Halo. Xbox. Pickup games of basketball. Mountain biking. Skiing. Football and fantasy football. Competing with each other is as easy as their playful (but mean-sounding) bantering.

> *Boys … treated friendship the way they treated the sun: its existence undisputed; its radiance best enjoyed, not beheld directly.*
>
> Khaled Hosseini, *A Thousand Splendid Suns*

Their souls are deep waters. Their feelings get hurt. They long to be respected. Believed in. Told they are strong. They need the validation of their masculine hearts. And as with yours, it needs to come from their heavenly Father.

Most young men haven't had their questions answered in the way they were meant to. Your heart has been wounded and so has theirs. Just as your heart has been wounded in the core of your femininity, theirs has been wounded in deeply masculine ways. With a heart that has deep, unaddressed questions, it's an easy temptation for a young man to hand over the validation of his life to the girl. He makes *as big a mistake* when he looks to a young woman to tell him he's got what it takes as you do when you look to him to tell you you're captivating. But most young men don't know that yet.

Be kind to them. Encourage their strength. Point them to Jesus. Treat their heart with respect and be mindful of your effect on them. It's greater than you realize.

Still, I think they should come with a warning label. Here's some of what it might read:

> I am not a girl. Don't confuse me with your girlfriend.
>
> I'm not as mature as you think I am.
>
> I don't know how to handle your heart.
>
> I'm sexually more quickly aroused than you are.
>
> I'm as insecure as you are, but I wear it differently.
>
> Don't allow me to be the verdict on you as a young woman.
>
> I'm visually stimulated, and when you wear that tight-fitting, low-cut number, I want to get my hands all over you. But if you let me, don't think for a minute that means I love you or will even remember your name.
>
> I live under the weight of peer pressure, and it causes me to say and do things that are not true to who I am or will become.
>
> I need to learn how to treat women with respect, and I need you to show me how by respecting yourself.

My emotions run deep and if I fall in love with
you, you have the capacity to break my heart
into many pieces. Please don't.

The best way to love me is to love God first and
bring to him the deepest questions and longings
of your heart.

*What else should the warning label say? And while we're
on the subject, if you came with a warning label, what
would it say? Fragile? Beware? Handle with care?*

can you trust him?

I read an article recently that said the way you can really know
what someone is like is by observing how they treat people in the
service industry. It's a good litmus test. The way of love is never
rude. Not to friends, siblings, parents, or waitresses. How we
treat others reveals so much about the quality of our character. If
you are drawn to a guy, before you move forward in the relationship, there are some litmus tests to see if you should. How we
live when we think no one is watching reveals the truth about
who we really are.

How does he treat others? What kind of friends does he have?
That says a lot about a person. What does he do for others? Does he
offer to help in any way? Or is life all about him? Is he pursuing a
relationship with Jesus? Do you like his friends? Are they good guys?
Most importantly, does he live with respect—does he treat others
with respect? Does he treat himself with respect? If not, there is no

way he will treat you with respect. You want to make sure you can trust the guy.

My husband and I wrote a book on marriage called *Love and War*. In it, we said that we believe we are here on earth to learn how to love. To really learn how to love. Love God. Love others. Love ourselves. And that's a tough thing to learn and requires a lifetime to do it well. Still, all throughout our lives, we get to grow in learning how to love! We get the honor of partnering with God in loving others. We get to grow in knowing how deeply he loves us each and every day. Love! Yay!

We are meant to be loved, to know love, and to love. When we do love others, we risk being hurt by them. Getting hurt happens. The only way not to be hurt is … well, there is no way. In *The Four Loves,* C. S. Lewis wrote,

> To love at all is to be vulnerable. Love anything, and your heart will certainly be wrung and possibly be broken. If you want to make sure of keeping it intact, you must give your heart to no one, not even to an animal. Wrap it carefully round with hobbies and little luxuries; avoid all entanglements; lock it up safe in the casket or coffin of your selfishness. But in that casket—safe, dark, motionless, airless— it will change. It will not be broken; it will become unbreakable, impenetrable, irredeemable.[1]

Yes, to love is to be vulnerable. We get hurt, misunderstood, wounded, and even betrayed. To keep on being women who love, we will need to be women who grow in wisdom and who continue to forgive. If you've been hurt by young men, God calls you to forgive them. That doesn't mean you stay in relationship with them. It means you forgive them, release them, and invite Jesus to heal you and help you learn.

Dear God, my heart is hurting. I'm hurt so much by what _____ did. But because I love you and you command me to, because you know what's best for me and know that I need to, because you have forgiven me, I forgive him. I forgive him for _____. I release him to you. I forgive myself for _____. Jesus, wash my wounded heart with your blood. Cleanse me again from every sin and stain and bleeding place. Speak to me here. I need to know your love again. Here. Thank you that your blood on the cross is enough to cleanse me from every sin I've committed and every sin that's been committed against me. You are enough. I love you. And, Jesus, I also sever all soul ties with _____. I bring your cross and your blood between me and _____. I release him to you. In Jesus's name I pray. Amen.

confounding

Guys can be confounding.

> confound—to cause surprise or confusion in (someone), especially by acting against their expectations[2]

These are tricky years you are living in, years to invite Jesus into every day. You can't navigate the waters of your heart, your relationships, or your life on your own. You are not meant to. You do not have to. The Holy Spirit is not only your strength and your comforter. He is your very own counselor sent to you by God because—well, because we all need one. Not every now and again but every moment of our lives. "I will pray the Father, and he will give you another Counselor, to be with you for ever" (John 14:16 RSV).

You are God's treasure. You are the center of his affection. He loves you deeply. He wants you to know it, live like it, and treat others the same way. Even those boys. And very likely, one day, one particular boy. Ask for his help to do it. Because helping you is what he loves to do.

Chapter Eleven

extravagant love

Love extravagantly.
1 Cor. 13:13 MSG

Our dog, Oban, loves me best.

He's a five-year-old golden retriever, and I'm his favorite. He pouts when I'm not home and stays in his cozy crate, uninterested in the happenings of the day—though not all that much is happening during the quiet of the weekday hours. But still he pouts. When I am home, Oban follows me around and lies down at my feet wherever I happen to be sitting: in the living-room chair, at my desk, or at the kitchen table. He's at my feet even now.

Oban follows me around because he adores me. And although I'd like to believe my dog's affection has absolutely nothing to do with the fact that I am the only one who feeds him, I know it has everything to do with it. Oban's attentiveness is simply him loving me in response to the way I have loved him and hoping that I may at any moment love him again by way of a biscuit.

Oban is a very smart dog. He knows where it will benefit him the most to focus his attention. We are, all of us, way smarter than my dog. Jesus has captured our attention, and now we want to sit at his feet.

what Jesus longs for

What is it that Jesus wants? What does he want more than anything else? Well, that's an easy one because he hasn't exactly kept it a secret. Jesus wants us to love him. Remember when Jesus was asked, "Which is the greatest commandment?" (Matt. 22:36). He answered, "Love the Lord your God with all your heart and with all your soul and with all your mind" (v. 37). Love God! Jesus is God. He is saying, "Love me! The most important and highest thing you can do with all of your life is to love me!"

Here's a fascinating thing: you reflect the heart of God. You are made in his image, right? Down to your feminine core, you express something about the heart of God to the world. And what does every woman's heart long for? To be loved. To be chosen. To be a priority to someone. Think of how deeply this runs in you. Now you know something really central about the heart of God. He wants that too.

Voluntarily offering our love to God is the most important thing we can do. Loving Jesus is the fire that fuels every other good work in our lives. And loving God enables us to live a courageous life that can't help but spill out onto others. Let's look into the Scriptures and learn from a woman who loved God first and with everything she had: Mary of Bethany.

Mary of Bethany was Lazarus's sister. The other half of Mary and Martha. She knew Jesus well. And because she knew him well, she loved him much. (Loving Jesus is simply the heart's natural response to knowing him.)

Now, in this story Martha represents a busy and distracted church. She is a picture of us when we have exchanged relationship with Jesus for service of him.

> As Jesus and his disciples were on their way, he came to a village where a woman named Martha opened her home to him. She had a sister called Mary, who sat at the Lord's feet listening to what he said. But Martha was distracted by all the preparations that had to be made. She came to him and asked, "Lord, don't you care that my sister has left me to do the work by myself? Tell her to help me!"
>
> "Martha, Martha," the Lord answered, "you are worried and upset about many things, but few things are needed—or indeed only one. Mary has chosen what is better, and it will not be taken away from her." (Luke 10:38–42)

Martha criticized her sister and rebuked the Lord. "Why are you just sitting there? Do you not see what is going on here? I am working so hard, and my sister is doing nothing. Make her help me." I love how Jesus gently corrected Martha for her worry and distraction. He didn't say that what Martha was doing was wrong, but that her attitude was. (Probably a good clue that we may be off in our attitudes is when we feel compelled to rebuke God for not intervening!)

But Mary's focus was undivided. She wasn't being lazy. She'd been captured. She wasn't running about helping her sister, because she was smitten with Jesus. She had chosen to learn from Jesus, to listen to his words, to open her heart and her mind to him. She was doing the one thing that was required—loving Jesus. And Jesus applauded her choice.

My family says I have ruined Oban because of my habit of giving him samples of what I'm eating. He loves to share an apple with me. A bite for me, a chunk for him. Oban isn't a very picky eater. He will eat anything. And by anything, I do mean anything. Dirty socks are a favorite. But above all Oban wants what the people around him are eating. So now, when others are eating, particularly if it is an apple, Oban will sit at their feet as well, eyes glued to their food, utterly and completely focused. He is captured. And maybe it's not the most flattering picture, but he reminds me of Mary. Nothing is going to distract that dog from the most important thing that is going on around him! He will sit with the undivided focus of a passionate disciple.

Mary sat at Jesus's feet, which is the sign of a disciple. (I love how Jesus was with women! It was scandalous at that time and remains scandalous in so many places today to have a woman disciple. But Jesus had them. He esteemed women.) Rather than being busy doing things for him, Mary was simply being with him. And Jesus said that being with him, listening to him, honoring him with her attention and adoration was far above doing things for him. "Martha, Martha … Mary has chosen what is better, and it will not be taken away from her."

Jesus defended Mary's choice. He didn't get angry with Martha either, by the way. He simply invited her to the better choice by presenting it to her.

Jesus doesn't pant after our service, as wonderful as it is. As much as he has planted desires and dreams in our hearts, he doesn't give first place to the use of our gifts to further the kingdom of God or to minister to his beloved lambs. Jesus says that the greatest command is to love him. We love him by loving others, yes, but God gives first place to our loving him, and we do that simply by being with him, spending time with him, fixing our gaze on who he is.

You know that when you really love someone, it gives you great joy just to be in the same room with them. Our sons no longer live at home, and when they do come home for a visit, I am so happy! Just to have them under the same roof as me makes me glad. My heart rests in the joy of their proximity. You know this. Mary knew this. Jesus knows this too.

i love you, i trust you

One of the next times we encounter Mary of Bethany in the Scriptures is after the death of her cherished brother, Lazarus. Jesus loved Lazarus. He loved Mary and Martha, too, but he didn't rush to Lazarus's side when he heard that he was sick. Jesus chose to wait two more days before traveling to Bethany. The sisters wanted him to come and heal Lazarus. But Jesus had something even better in mind.

So he waited. And then he performed one of the greatest miracles of his earthly ministry. Just as we have had to do so many times, Mary and Martha had to wait for God to come. Waiting for God is one of the hardest things we ever have to do, isn't it? But if Jesus had come right away and healed Lazarus, we all would have missed out.

What are you asking Jesus to do? What are you waiting for?

Believing God is good in the midst of waiting is incredibly hard. Believing God is good in the midst of immense sorrow, loss, or pain is even more difficult. Those are the times when our faith, the treasure of our hearts, is tested by fire and becomes gold. What we come to know of God and the terrain he comes to inhabit in our hearts through the trial leads people to say, "I wouldn't change a thing." That's the crazy, supernatural realm of God.

I know there are times when God didn't answer your prayers in the way you wanted or in the timing you wanted. But what he did in the end was far better. Even if the "far better" was your coming to depend on him more deeply through the travail.

All of us are living lives that are wondrous and filled with heartaches. That is real. I can only imagine what you are living in … waiting for … longing for … weeping for. Holding on to your faith for. I know what I am living in. Gold is being forged, girls. Priceless, immeasurable gold. To paraphrase Philip Yancey: faith believes ahead of time what can be seen only by looking back.[1] There will come a day when we will look back and understand. But in the waiting, may God strengthen our hearts to hold on to his.

Lazarus had been dead for four days when Jesus finally came to town. And I love that when Martha heard he had come, she ran out to meet him. Martha may get a raw deal sometimes, but she was running to him in this moment. She loved Jesus. She said, "Lord … if you had been here, my brother would not have died" (John 11:21). And then she said,

> "But I know that even now God will give you whatever you ask." …
>
> Jesus said to her, "I am the resurrection and the life. The one who believes in me will live, even though they die; and whoever lives by believing in me will never die. Do you believe this?"
>
> "Yes, Lord," she replied, "I believe that you are the Messiah, the Son of God, who is to come into the world." (vv. 22, 25–27)

Theologians call this the threefold confession. It was the highest confession that Martha could make. Yay, Martha! And don't you love how she said, "But I know that even now God will give you whatever you ask"? Martha was still holding out her hope for the miraculous intervention of Jesus.

Mary didn't come. She stayed in the house, grieving. She didn't go to Jesus until she was told that he was asking after her. Mary was a real person. She wasn't this amazing I-do-it-right-all-the-time gal. She was a woman like you and me who, when overcome by grief, sometimes cannot even move. Mary couldn't move, not until she was called out by her God.

Mary loved Jesus. She ran to him then and fell at his feet. She worshipped him. She brought to Jesus the whole truth of who she was, including her profound grief and uncontrolled weeping. And in seeing her weeping, the Scripture says, Jesus was "deeply moved" (v. 33). Jesus was moved by the heartfelt tears of one who loved him, and he is moved by yours as well.

Did you hear me? Jesus is moved by your tears, your love, your waiting, and your sorrows. He is moved when you trust him even though it all looks hopeless. It is one of the deepest ways we express our love for him.

Martha and Mary laid out their hearts before Jesus. And they chose to trust him. You know what happened next!

Do you have a story of a time when God did not come in the way or the timing that you had wanted, but what unfolded was even better than you had hoped? What happened?

lavish loving

Days later, when Jesus was again having dinner with the very much alive Lazarus (Jesus had raised him from the dead) and Martha was … well, serving, Mary did the unthinkable. She came quietly into the room with an alabaster jar of very expensive perfume. (And by the way, she wasn't at home. She was at Simon the Leper's house. Mary brought the oil with her. She planned this ahead of time!)

Many commentators believe this perfume was her life savings. Mary broke the neck of the jar open and slowly poured some of the perfume on Jesus's head and then poured the rest on his feet. Then she did something extremely intimate and scandalous. She unbound her hair and wiped his feet with it, even though a respectable woman did not let down her hair in public.

Mary was not concerned with what anyone else thought. She had an undivided heart. She poured out all she had onto Jesus in an extravagant offering of worship. She spent herself on him. She ministered to him in a culturally significant way. Nowadays, pouring all of your Chanel No. 5 onto someone you think highly of might well end that relationship, but what Mary did was a recognizable offering of worship.

There were several immediate results.

First, the fragrance of her offering filled the room. There was a *change in the atmosphere.* When we pour out all we have in worship to Jesus, the beauty of that offering can be sensed by those around us. It is an alluring fragrance that lingers.

Early in Acts, the Pharisees were amazed at the courage of Peter and John. Peter and John spoke with power, and the Pharisees noted that these men had been with Jesus. When we worship Jesus, when we are with him, the fragrance of his love fills our hearts and spills over. The atmosphere changes within us and around us. Just as the Pharisees could tell, people can tell that we have been with Jesus.

The second thing that happened after Mary ministered to Jesus was that the disciples rebuked her. Over and over again, Jesus had told his disciples that he would be killed in Jerusalem and then rise. But they didn't understand. The opposition to Jesus was growing stronger every day. There was a contract out on his life. He was being hunted. It was attentive Mary who sat at the Lord's feet who knew there was not much time left. There was nothing Mary owned that she would not spend on him.

The gospel tells us that those present were indignant and rebuked her harshly. *What a waste of money! A whole year's wages poured out for nothing! Think of how many poor families could eat for a week on that.* They saw only money. Mary saw only Jesus.

Have you ever had your motives misunderstood? Have you ever had someone criticize the way you dress or spend your time or money, the way you believe or come through or don't come through? It has happened to me countless times, and I hate it. Jesus isn't so fond of it either. When people judge you, that is. Especially for loving him. Jesus knows well that it hurts to be misunderstood and judged. He knows that it is part of the sorrow of living in a fallen world.

We hurt others when we interpret their actions through lenses of misunderstanding wrought in our brokenness and sin. We are hurt by others when they do it to us. And when it happens to us, how are we supposed to defend ourselves? What did Mary do? Well, Mary didn't say a word in her own defense—but Jesus did. Jesus always defends a worshipper. Sometimes God will ask us to speak—in love—but always he is our Defender.

> "Leave her alone," said Jesus. "Why are you bothering her? She has done a beautiful thing to me. The poor you will always have with you, and you can help them any time you want. But you will not always have me. She did what she could. She poured perfume on my body beforehand to

prepare for my burial. Truly I tell you, wherever
the gospel is preached throughout the world, what
she has done will also be told, in memory of her."
(Mark 14:6–9)

Jesus defended Mary's reckless devotion. Jesus "got" Mary, and
he "gets" you. He understood her heart and the depth of her love.
He said, "She has done a beautiful thing to me." He never said that
about anyone or anything else. What was the beautiful thing? She
spent all her love on him.

But did you notice what else Jesus said? "She did what she
could." She had her unique portion, and she gave it all. There is
grace here for us to receive, girls. We are not the same. Comparing
ourselves to one another leads to death. We are each given a portion. We are given our part to play. We are a body. We need each
other. *We do what we can.*

The Gospels don't mention this Mary again. She wasn't at the
crucifixion or the empty tomb. This Mary, who was inside her
home grieving the loss of her brother, Lazarus, after his death and
unable to run to meet Jesus, is the same woman who knew that
Jesus was going to die—and believed he was going to be raised on
the third day. But her heart could not take seeing it happen.

Although Mary wasn't physically there, her offering of love
was. The fragrance of the oil Mary had poured out on Jesus days
before was still on his hair, his feet, and wherever else it dripped.
Mary wasn't at the crucifixion, but the beauty of her offering was.

Mary understood the times, she had amazing faith, and she
ministered to Jesus in a way that no one else even comprehended,

because she knew him. She loved him. She worshipped him extravagantly.

And Jesus *loved* it.

> *Mary poured out her offering of love and worship to Jesus via her life savings of precious nard. She loved him recklessly. What might it look like for you to offer Jesus your worship recklessly? What would you like to pour out on Jesus?*

Mary chose Jesus above all else. Have you ever been chosen? Over lots of other people? Picked first for the dodgeball team? Asked to a dance? Selected for the cheer squad? Given a choice role in the school play? Been the recipient of an award? It is a wonderful thing to be chosen.

Growing up, I wasn't athletic. I was never picked first for the team, and I was never asked to a dance. However, when I was in the fourth grade, I was chosen by my classmates to be Citizen of the Year. I still remember the joy of it. Each day the teacher chose one student to be Citizen of the Day. Their name went up on the special chart for all to see. On the last day of school the teacher tallied up the names to see who had won the honor most often. It turned out to be a tie between me and a cute boy named Bobby. So she took a private vote. The thing was, there were more boys in the classroom than girls, so I was pretty certain I wouldn't win.

But I had an edge. My family was moving in a week or so from our home in Prairie Village, Kansas, to unknown California. I was leaving, and everyone knew it. This could be my good-bye present. And I did win.

At the time I thought it was a sympathy vote, or it could have been that I was just more citizenly than he was. But I didn't really care why I won. I simply cared that *I* was chosen. My prize was a certificate and the cardboard sheet with the school photos of all my classmates. I took their photos off the board, put them in an envelope, and brought them with me to California.

I was chosen immediately before a separation from my friends and caregivers in what would become the earthquake of my young life. When we got to our new state, my family utterly fell apart. How many times did I go to my little box and pour over my classmates' pictures and remember that I was loved and that there was a place where people knew and cared for me? I had been chosen. It was a God-given lifeline of remembrance when I needed it most.

You have been chosen too.

> You did not choose me, but I chose you. (John 15:16)

> For he chose us in him before the creation of the world. (Eph. 1:4)

> God's chosen people, holy and dearly loved. (Col. 3:12)

It is important for us to let our hearts rest in that. It is so important that we remember that we are loved. We, too, have been chosen.

love as worship

One of the best ways to help us remember who our God is and who we are to him is to worship him. In worship, when we turn the gaze of our hearts away from ourselves and our needs and onto Jesus, a divine shift happens that brings a great good to our lives. Our enormous struggles and concerns become much less overwhelming in the face of our powerful, loving Jesus. In worship, we remember that we have been bought with his precious blood. We remember who we belong to.

You are Jesus's beloved: "I belong to my beloved, and his desire is for me" (Song of Sol. 7:10). He cares for you and those you love beyond telling. You are forever loved.

Worshipping him is our opportunity to love him in response. It is our response to being loved, forgiven, and known. It is our chance to offer our thanks for being seen, chosen, wanted, understood, cherished, and made new! Worship is our response to seeing Jesus as he really is: worthy, beautiful, endlessly good, kind, forgiving, generous, wonderful, and utterly, completely *for* us.

Worship is an intimate encounter with God that changes us by aligning our spirits with truth even when it doesn't *feel* true. We pour ourselves out onto him, and he pours himself into us. It is a divine exchange that ministers to his heart and renews our own.

Our worship of Jesus pushes back the kingdom of darkness and ushers in the kingdom of God. It changes the atmosphere around us so that others can sense, *These were with Jesus.*

Intimate worship is simply telling God how wonderful he is and why. It is pouring out our love onto him like oil. We bring him all that we are, even our weariness and sorrow. *Jesus, I give you my weariness. I give you my doubt. I give you my desire to give up. I come with my need. I offer you my desire, my gifting, my weakness, my hope, my everything. I give you all that I am, God. I give you my love.* In our loving of Jesus we become increasingly available for him to continue his deep work in us, transforming us into the women we long to be.

Worshipping Jesus enables us to be like Mary of Bethany and to minister to Jesus with our adoration, our tears, and our thankful hearts. Why don't you take a few minutes and come before him now?

Jesus is worthy of our devotion and our thanks. Your Jesus is the One who rode into the depths of the darkest, most dangerous dungeon to rescue his true love. He is the One who will ride again on a white steed with fire in his eyes and a flaming sword in his hand. He has inscribed you into the palm of his nail-pierced hand. He knows your every thought, numbers your every hair, and cherishes your every tear. Jesus weeps for you and with you, longs for you, hopes for you, dreams of you, and rejoices over you with singing. He is the One who has battled all the forces of hell to free you and who battles still.

Jesus is your knight in shining armor. He is the love you have been longing for. He is your dream come true. He is your hero. He is Aslan, the Lion of Judah, and the Lamb of God. He is the Prince of Peace, the Alpha and Omega, the First and the Last, the King of Kings and the Lord of Lords, the Mighty One.

His name is like a kiss and an earthquake. His gaze is on you. He has pledged his love to you and betrothed you to him forever. He is unchangeable, and his love will never fail you.

How will you respond? Love him. Adore him. Worship him.

God is inviting us to become a woman like Mary of Bethany, who knew that our greatest treasure is Jesus and his greatest pleasure is our worship.

> *Have a time of intimate worship. Remember, intimate worship is simply telling God how wonderful he is and why. It is pouring out our love onto him like oil. We bring him all that we are: our love, our hope, even our weariness and sorrow. Take twenty minutes, play anointed worship music in the background, and practice coming before Jesus just to love on him. He will love it!*

Chapter Twelve

your true name

Tell me who admires and loves you, and I will tell you who you are.

Antoine de Saint-Exupéry

I love a good fairy tale. Give me a "happily ever after" any day of the week. Glass slippers, the power of love's first kiss, good triumphing over evil, and everyone's true nature being revealed (She's a dragon! She's a princess!) all make my heart glad. So naturally, the royal wedding of Prince William and Kate Middleton captured my imagination. It was a fairy-tale wedding played out before the world.

An estimated two billion people across the earth watched the nuptials of Will and Kate. It seems the whole world was mesmerized. Lovely Kate was born a "commoner," but now she is married to the son of Prince Charles, the future prince of Wales and future king of England. *People* magazine published a special issue that trumpeted on the cover, "Love Reigns!" Yes! In some deep place, we all long for transcendence; we long for fairy tales to be true!

stolen identity

The heir to the British throne has been given the title "Prince of Wales" since the twelve hundreds when King Edward (remember Longshanks from *Braveheart?*—that's the one) conquered the wild and noble Welsh and took from them their land, their laws, and their language. He and those after him couldn't quite do it, though. Eight hundred years later, the language, the unique history, and the flavor of Wales remain.

I confess I have a bit of a crush on Llywelyn the Great. This Prince of Wales was the first to truly unite the country. Much of his life is a picture of Jesus to me, and I don't know why Hollywood has not figured out the glorious story there and made a movie about him, but they should. (Have your people call my people!)

Anyway, he was a nobleman whose grandson and namesake— known as Llywelyn the Last—followed in his grandfather's footsteps and tried to unite, lead, and protect Wales. His life is a noble story as well, but a sad one. He was killed in a small skirmish and was unable to save his country from the English invasion that changed the little country's destiny.

Llywelyn the Last had one heir—a baby girl. She was only months old when Wales fell to the English, but since she was an infant and a female, her fate was not as bad as it would have been had she been a boy. She was captured by Edward's troops, and the king interned her at Sempringham Priory in England for the rest of her life. She eventually became a nun in her thirties and died twenty years later, knowing little of her heritage and speaking none of her native language.

Her name was Gwenllian. I don't know how to say it correctly, but no one else ever did either. Not to her. The English couldn't pronounce it, so they simplified it. She was a princess in exile, living in a land ruled by her father's enemy. The ache in her heart for her true home was most likely never understood and certainly never fulfilled. She never left the confines of the nunnery her entire life.

The Welsh have a word for the ache in one's heart for her true home, for the longing that goes deeper than understanding: *hiraeth*. It is a holy word for a holy ache.

Gwenllian lived with that ache. She was meant to reign, but her throne was stolen. She was stripped of her authority and lived her life in captivity, never knowing her true identity, never hearing her true name.

Can you imagine being royalty but being treated like a servant? Can you imagine being the daughter of the true king but being held in low regard and never setting foot in your home country for as long as you live? Can you imagine being destined to reign yet never even hearing your true name? Of course you can. The parallels are astonishing. Truly.

Would it have made a difference for Gwenllian if she had known the truth? Would it have mattered in her life, in her heart, if she had known who her father was? Who she was? Does it make a difference in ours? Oh yes. It makes all the difference in the world.

Let us, then, remember who we truly are. Let us go further up and further in to all the riches and the joy and the intimacy and the healing that God has for us! Do you remember who you are? Whose you are?

First, **you are the daughter of the King.** You are your Father's delight. You are the apple of his eye and the one on whom his affections rest.

Second, **you are the bride of Christ.** You are engaged to the High Prince. You are the beloved of Jesus. There is a royal wedding coming, unparalleled in the history of men and angels, and all the eyes of creation will be riveted and rejoicing.

Third, **you are the ally-friend of Jesus**. You were sent to this earth to bring about the invasion by his kingdom. You have a role in a mighty story filled with beauty and danger.

When we believe something is true, it affects the choices we make. We believe gravity exists, so we jump up, safe in the knowledge that we will come down again. We believe the sun will rise, so we go to bed without the fear that night will last forever. But sometimes—actually quite often—God calls us to believe something before we experientially know it. The popular saying is "seeing is believing," but in Christ, believing leads to seeing. God invites us to believe we are who he says we are. Regardless of our experience.

what's in a name?

What you name something is immeasurably important.

There is power in what we name ourselves. There is power in what other people name us as well. Both the power to bless and the power to curse come from the heart and flow out of the mouth through words. What we call something, what we are called, whether good or evil, will play itself out in our lives. The following article is a perfect real-life example.

> More than 200 Indian girls whose names mean "unwanted" in Hindi have chosen new names for a fresh start in life.

A central Indian district held a renaming ceremony Saturday that it hopes will give the girls new dignity and help fight widespread gender discrimination that gives India a skewed gender ratio, with far more boys than girls.

The 285 girls—wearing their best outfits with barrettes, braids and bows in their hair—lined up to receive certificates with their new names along with small flower bouquets from Satara district officials in Maharashtra state.

In shedding names like "Nakusa" or "Nakushi," which mean "unwanted" in Hindi, some girls chose to name themselves after Bollywood stars such as "Aishwarya." ... Some just wanted traditional names with happier meanings, such as "Vaishali" or "prosperous, beautiful and good."

"Now in school, my classmates and friends will be calling me this new name, and that makes me very happy," said a 15-year-old girl who had been named Nakusa by a grandfather disappointed by her birth.[1]

Isn't that beautiful? And horrible? And vitally important?

What names do you call yourself? When you pass a mirror? When you blow it?

What you call someone or something is powerful. What you are called affects your life, your relationships, and your walk with God. What you call yourself *affects your ability to become who you are meant to be*. God knows there is power in what we call ourselves. Knowing this, listen to the fierce intention of God, who says he will change *your* name:

> Because I love Zion [insert your name here],
>   I will not keep still.
> Because my heart yearns for [her],
>   I cannot remain silent.
> I will not stop praying for her
>   until her righteousness shines like the
>   dawn,
>   and her salvation blazes like a burning
>   torch.
> The nations will see your righteousness.
>   World leaders will be blinded by your
>   glory.
> And you will be given a new name
>   by the Lord's own mouth.
> The Lord will hold you in his hand for all
>   to see—
>   a splendid crown in the hand of God.
> Never again will you be called "The
>   Forsaken City"
>   or "The Desolate Land."

> Your new name will be "The City of God's
> Delight"
> and "The Bride of God,"
> for the LORD delights in you
> and will claim you as his bride. (Isa.
> 62:1–4 NLT)

This beautiful passage comes after Isaiah 61, which promises your healing and restoration and your deliverance from the Enemy. Now God promises a new name. No longer will you be called Deserted but Sought After. You are not unwanted. You are pursued. You are worth pursuing, chasing after, romancing. You are wanted.

God wants us to name things correctly, including ourselves. It's vitally important that we do.

> I belong to my beloved,
> and his desire is for me. (Song of Sol.
> 7:10)

God names you "beloved." What does beloved mean? It means one greatly loved, dear to the heart. It means admired, adored, cherished, darling. Beloved means dear, dear one, dearest, esteemed, favorite, honey. It means ladylove, light of love, loved one, lover, precious, prized, respected, and revered. Beloved means you. *It means who you are to him. And who you are to him means everything.*

God calls you to believe it. He wants you to know who you are. You need to.

The fruit of knowing who you are to Christ is intimacy with him. It isn't walking around all puffed up. *Oh, look at me! I'm something special!* The fruit is neither pride nor arrogance. The fruit is humility. It is surrendered gratefulness. The fruit of believing we are who God says we are is a deepening love for Jesus. We love because he first loved us. Belief evokes a response; we choose to draw near to this God who prizes us. And that is exactly what God is after.

So who are you?

Well, you may be like me, and it's hard for me to answer this question with grace when I just got so irritated with my husband that I had to leave the room. God sees me as lovely, but lovely thoughts have not been filling my mind just now. I need help! When we believe that our truest identity is a sinner, then we walk around ashamed, accused, condemned. Separated from God. Which does not make for a happy camper and which is exactly where our Enemy, the Devil, wants us to live. The Devil is called the accuser of the brethren for a reason.

Hang on a sec; I need to go apologize to my husband …

Okay, I'm back. When the focus of our hearts is solely on our failings, then our hearts spiral down. God tells us not to focus on our failings but on his faithfulness. He calls us to gaze not on our brokenness but on our Healer. He says we should "[fix] our eyes on Jesus, the pioneer and perfecter of faith" (Heb. 12:2). We move toward what we focus on.

We are warned in Scripture not to think more highly of ourselves than we ought, but honestly that is a rare woman. I have yet to meet that woman. But I have met a lot of women who think much less of themselves than they ought. Certainly much less than

God does. And that is not only disheartening; it is dangerous. Why? Because you cannot live well, you cannot love well, and you cannot fulfill your destiny if you do not know who you are.

You cannot become yourself if you do not know who you are to become.

scoreboard

My friend's son Gannon is a superb soccer player. As a freshman in high school, he helped lead the varsity team to the state championship. He is a quiet, polite young man who transforms into a warrior once he hits the field. During one of his recent games, he had an opportunity to believe.

Gannon's team was in the lead by three goals, a massive lead in soccer. Guarding him was a player who used insults to try to keep Gannon from being his glorious soccer-playing self. They call it "talking smack." He was incessant. Mean.

"You are the worst player on this team." "You can't even kick the ball." "No one on your team likes you." "You shouldn't be on this team." "You're just a baby freshman." "Go home, little boy." Sound familiar? "You're blowing it. You can't do this well at all. You never will. You're not qualified. You don't have any real friends. You should just go home."

What do you hear inside you when you forget a friend's birthday? Hurt someone's feelings? Find out you weren't invited to the party? Gain three pounds? Sin?

Gannon's accuser didn't take a break. He started right in again after every time-out. Gannon said it was the most difficult thing he had ever endured on the field. "You missed! You are always going to miss." Accusations hurt. Spiritual warfare hurts.

Gannon didn't engage him in a verbal battle. He didn't entertain the accusations coming against him or defend himself. He merely answered him, "Scoreboard." That is all he ever replied. "Scoreboard." His accuser could say what he wanted; there was no silencing him. But Gannon's team was winning the game. He and his teammates were playing well. The truth lay in the scoreboard. Gannon's defense lay in the truth. There was no catching them. You bet they won that game. Now, that silenced his accuser.

Scoreboard. Done and done. Jesus has won our victory, and we are victorious as well, in him. We are not defined by our sin, our failures, or our past. We are forever and only defined by the finished work of Jesus Christ. Everything Jesus did and won was for us. We were slaves to sin, yes. But because of Jesus, we are slaves no longer. We are daughters. We are brides.

Who do you think you are? Really.

Though the author is unknown, I love the following quote. It helps me realize that there are tangible ramifications to my thoughts. They matter. There is an effect.

Watch your thoughts, for they become words.
Watch your words, for they become actions.
Watch your actions, for they become habits. Watch

your habits, for they become your character. And
watch your character, for it becomes your destiny!
What we think, we become.

What we think, we become.

In the midst of your day—in the mess, the mundane, the
glorious—when you laugh and live well and when you don't, it is so
good to get into the habit of stopping and asking yourself, *Is what I
am thinking about myself true?* If it does not line up with the Word of
God, reject it as a lie. Replace it with the truth.

What would it be like right now to entertain the possibility in
your heart that all God says about you is true?

You are his delight.

You make him happy just by being you.

He thinks you're lovely.

You are his beloved.

You are the one who has captured his heart.

What difference would it make in your life if it really was true?
Think of it. Let your heart go there for a moment. Because it does
make all the difference in the world.

You must ask him: *Am I your beloved? How do you see me? Do you
delight in me? Do you love me because you're God and that's your job, or
do you love me simply for me?*

> *This is so vitally important and it has to be personal. We
> need to know who we are to God. So then, we must ask
> him. Ask God. Right now.*

You, dear heart, you are the beloved.

Jesus, thank you for this truth about me. I receive it. I agree with you, and I declare that I am your daughter. I am chosen, holy, and dearly loved. I am the apple of your eye. I am your beloved, and your desire is for me. Please, write this truth deeply in my heart. In Jesus's name, I pray. Amen.

who you are

Have you ever had to go to an event that you didn't want to go to, a party or a game or a family gathering? I had a birthday party I needed to attend recently, and I wasn't very happy about it. I complained to my husband that I had to go and spend hours with people I had never met nor would ever see again. Blah blah blah. And John said, "Rename it. Call it good."

Riiiigghht—it's not evil; it's good. It's an opportunity to bless someone I care very much about. It's a chance to celebrate her life. I renamed it, changed my frame of reference, and went with a happy heart.

There are many things we need to rename in our lives. Our school experience. Our relationships. Even our life itself. Rename them. Rename your life. It's good. Because your life belongs to our good God, and he's got you. Rename yourself. *God has.*

My parents named me Stasi. It means resurrection. There is a lot in my life that has needed resurrecting over the years—my wounded heart, my damaged sexuality, my broken self-perception, my dreams, my relationships, my calling. And God is resurrecting every area of my life to *life*. He is resurrecting my mind to be able to believe that all he has made, and all he has made *me*, is good. He is resurrecting my dreams and my desires and even my yearning to be deeply known and perfectly loved. Yes, my parents named me Stasi, but really it was God who named me "Resurrection."

What's your given name? What does it mean?

Do you know what your given name means? It's a good idea to find out. And if you don't like the meaning you initially discover, press in to find out more about it. Ask God to reveal to you why he named you what he did. A friend of mine's name is Melanie. I asked her what it means, and with a little shrug she told me, "It means dark." Huh. Dark. We pressed in to find out more about what her name means and discovered it doesn't mean simply "dark." It means "dark beauty." In Hebrew it actually means "Grace-filled beauty." Song of Solomon says, "Dark am I, yet lovely" (1:5). Which can mean, "Yes, I am imperfect, and I see my many failings and sins, but when God looks at me, he sees my beauty, not my sin. To Jesus, I am and have only ever been lovely." That's what Melanie means. See, it's a good idea to find out.

Because whatever else is true about what you are named, God says:

No longer are you called Desolate, but Married.
No longer are you alone or unseen; your name is
    Sought After. Beloved. Mine.
No longer are you called Nakusa, Unwanted.
Your name is Vaishali—Prosperous, Beautiful,
    and Good.

As we journey on into becoming our true selves, we want to live with holy intention. We want to be awake to the present moment, those around us, the Spirit within us, and our own souls. We are meant to live lives of significance. It is right that we desire to live for a purpose higher than protecting our skin from sun damage and being well liked. We want to live unto a high calling, a meaningful purpose, and that purpose flows out of our identity.

Knowing who we are enables us to live the life we have been born to live—the life the seen and unseen world needs us to live. We need to know who we are and own who we are. Who are you? What is your identity—really?

You are a new creation in Christ, more than a conqueror. Victorious. Strong. Empowered. Safe. Secure. Sealed. You are a channel of the life and love of God. You are alive in Christ. You are the beloved of God. You are his.

Who is Jesus? He is the love you have been longing for all your life, and he has never taken his eyes off of you. He has a name for you that he wants you to fully become; he holds your true identity, and this is what you are meant to grow into. So go ahead and ask Jesus your true name (or names—he often has several for us).

Jesus, I choose to believe that I am your beloved and that your desire is for me. I choose to believe that I am no longer forsaken or deserted, but that I am your delight, sought after and dearly loved. Jesus, I want to become the young woman you have in mind for me to be. Show me who she is; show me who I really am, who I was always meant to be. Tell me my true name; give me an image of who you see me becoming. Give me eyes to see and ears to hear and the courage to accept what you are saying. Tell me, Jesus.

And as he does, dear one, choose to believe. Because who God says you are is who you are. And who you are is good.

> You will be called by a new name
> that the mouth of the LORD will bestow.
> (Isa. 62:2)

parting thoughts

Thank you for taking this journey with me. Though the book has ended, the journey certainly has not. Each and every one of us is still growing into the woman we want to be, the woman God created us to be. Our life is one of continual discovery and transformation. There are experiences to be had. There are choices to be made. There are truths to be believed. There is much to be learned. I'm still learning. So are you. We are on this road together, urged on by a great company of witnesses, seen and unseen. We are surrounded by love every moment of our lives. We are held in the gaze of the One who has won everything, done everything, and paid everything so that we might be free to live, free to love, and free to be ourselves. We are free to offer all that we are back to him in a life rich with joy, steeped in goodness, strengthened in hope, and abounding in love.

Jesus goes before you, behind you, and within you. You are never alone, and you will always have all that you need. Let's press on together.

> Now to him who is able to keep you from stumbling
> and to present you blameless before the presence of

his glory with great joy, to the only God, our Savior, through Jesus Christ our Lord, be glory, majesty, dominion, and authority, before all time and now and forever. (Jude vv. 24–25 ESV)

afterword

The journey of your life is well under way. Because you have read this book, I know you are a young woman who wants her life to be one of power and significance. You want to live with holy intention, becoming all you are meant to be, and to partner with Jesus in bringing his kingdom. I am so grateful. Know that you are not alone. You are being prayed for and cheered on by a great company of witnesses, including me.

I want to encourage you to stay engaged in the messages of *Free to Be Me*. This isn't the kind of book that you read and then simply toss aside for the next thing. This is the journey of your life, your growing in your knowledge that God is the key to living the life you are meant to live. Let the messages and themes in this book marinate in your heart. There is more life to be had. There is more healing, more freedom, and more joy!

Come visit my Stasi Eldredge Facebook page! I'll be posting blogs and videos and just sharing life with you.

Ransomed Heart—our ministry—is a treasure trove of resources. We're a little band devoted to Jesus, to bringing his kingdom and to restoring the hearts of men and women all over the world. We have so many resources to help you grow in your own becoming! Come visit us at www.ransomedheart.com. Sign up to receive the free (!) daily readings. Browse our store. Come to one of our conferences. Like us on Facebook. Read our blogs. Join with others who are on this path. Our desire is to strengthen the hearts of God's people. We want to introduce Jesus to folks who've never met him or who have a lower version of who he really is!

The more we know Jesus, the more we love him.. The more we love him, the more healed and the more ourselves we become. People actually will ask you for the reason for the hope that is within you! Jesus is the reason. He is so marvelous, and there is no end to discovering the beauty and majesty of his alluring heart. So let the adventure continue.

We're in it together!

With love and hope,

Stasi Eldredge

The LORD bless you and keep you; the LORD make his face shine on you and be gracious to you; the LORD turn his face toward you and give you peace.
Numbers 6:24–26

notes

chapter one: the heart of the matter

1. Dr. Seuss, *Happy Birthday to You!* (New York: Random House, 1959), 44.
2. John Eldredge, *Waking the Dead* (Nashville: Thomas Nelson, 2003), 40.
3. C. S. Lewis, *Mere Christianity* (New York: Macmillan, 1943, 1945, 1952), 190.

chapter two: what's your story?

1. George MacDonald, *The Diary of an Old Soul*, entry for June 16 (Minneapolis: Augsburg, 1965), 64.
2. Oswald Chambers, *My Utmost for His Highest: An Updated Edition in Today's Language* (Grand Rapids, MI: Discovery House, 1992).

chapter three: the landscape of your life

1. For more on these four seasons, I recommend *Emotional Phases of a Woman's Life* by Jean Lush and Patricia H. Rushford (Old Tappan, NJ: Revell, 1987).
2. "Ethiopian Girl Reportedly Guarded by Lions," NBCNews.com, June 21, 2005, www.nbcnews.com/id/8305836/ns/world_news-africa/t/ethiopian-girl-reportedly -guarded-lions/#.U4eiRPmICM4.

3. *Merriam-Webster OnLine*, s.v. "misogyny," accessed May 31, 2012, www.merriam-webster.com/dictionary/misogyny.

4. Michael Flood et al., eds., *International Encyclopedia of Men and Masculinities* (New York: Routledge, 2007), 443.

5. Jimmy Carter (@askjimmycarter), Twitter, May 5, 2014.

6. "The Crisis," compassion2one, http://www.compassion2one.org/content-pages/12814/d24aa06f-18ba-486b-bc03-89bbe8c6fe64/TheCrisis.aspx.

7. Julie Baumgardner, "Human Trafficking," Timesfreepress.com, April 15, 2012, www.timesfreepress.com/news/2012/apr/15/041512e2-human-trafficking/.

8. Julie Baumgardner, "First Things First: What About the Children?" Timesfreepress.com, April 1, 2012, http://www.timesfreepress.com/news/2012/apr/01/what-about-the-children/.

chapter four: your mother, yourself

1. Mark Salzman, "Jailhouse Bach," *Reader's Digest*, May 2004.

2. Becky, communication with the author. Used with permission.

chapter five: be you. not them.

1. Dan Zadra, *5: Where Will You Be Five Years from Today?* (Seattle: Compendium, 2009), 9.

chapter six: beauty secrets

1. Author unknown.

chapter seven: stumbling into freedom

1. *The Shawshank Redemption*, directed by Frank Darabont (Culver City, CA: Columbia Pictures, 1994), DVD.

2. Sabatina James, "Sabatina James: Why My Mother Wants Me Dead," *Newsweek*, March 5, 2012, http://www.newsweek.com/sabatina-james-why-my-mother-wants -me-dead-63709.

3. John Eldredge, *Waking the Dead* (Nashville: Thomas Nelson, 2003), 18.

4. For more on this, see Eldredge, *Waking the Dead*; and Neil T. Anderson, *The Bondage Breaker* (Eugene, OR: Harvest House, 1990).

chapter eight: a little rain

1. Sarah Young, *Jesus Calling* (Nashville: Integrity, 2004), 341.

chapter nine: friendship

1. "Boys and Girls Are Bullied Differently, from Ann Shoket," web video, MarloThomas.com/Huffington Post, September 27, 2013, www.huffingtonpost .com/2011/09/20/boys-and-girls-are-bullie_n_972144.html.

2. For more on this, see Andy Reese, *Freedom Tools: For Overcoming Life's Tough Problems* (Grand Rapids, MI: Chosen, 2008); and John Eldredge, *Waking the Dead* (Nashville: Thomas Nelson, 2003).

chapter ten: those boys!

1. C. S. Lewis, *The Four Loves* (New York: Harcourt Brace, 1960), 121.

2. Oxford Dictionaries, s.v. "confound," www.oxforddictionaries.com/us/definition /american_english/confound.

chapter eleven: extravagant love

1. Philip Yancey, *Where Is God When It Hurts?* (Grand Rapids, MI: Zondervan, 1990), 161.

chapter twelve: your true name

1. Chaya Babu, "285 Indian Girls Shed 'Unwanted' Names," Yahoo! News, October 22, 2011, http://news.yahoo.com/285-indian-girls-shed-unwanted-names -122551876.html.

God is a dreamer.
He has dreams of you.
And for you.

—stasi eldredge, *becoming myself*

This powerful series will take you deeper into your own story as you become the woman God desires you to be. Stasi ushers women into an authentic journey of freedom, healing, and transformation. Explore God's intimate involvement in your past and his unique dreams for your future.